ONCE THE STORM IS OVER

From grieving to healing after
the suicide of my daughter

by Nina Bingham

Nina Bingham

ISBN: 978-0-9908413-1-9

Printed in the United States of America

This book is based on actual events; however some names have been changed, and in some cases, composite characters have been created.

Cover photo: Selfie by Moriyah Jones
Author photo: Selfie by Nina Binham
Cover design: Ridge Studio

Big Table Publishing Company
Boston, MA
bigtablepublishing.com

ACKNOWLEDGMENTS

I would like to express my deepest gratitude to Robin Stratton at Big Table Publishing Company for her patient guidance, enthusiastic encouragement, and for making my book personal and engaging. Robin provided me with the confidence to believe in myself again.

I cannot express enough thanks to Adam Standridge at Ridge Studios for creating my book cover, trailer, and websites. His willingness to give his time and talent so generously has been very much appreciated.

I wish to acknowledge my mental health hero, Dr. Elyn R. Saks, esteemed professor, lawyer, and research psychoanalyst at the University of Southern California Law School, and best-selling author of *The Center Cannot Hold: My Journey Through Madness*. Her book kept me company in my darkest hours of grief, and her bravery helped me to find my voice again.

Gratitude to my sister Rhonda Spencer of Rhonda Spencer Design, who flew to my side in my darkest hour, and whose brilliant graphic direction makes me look more organized than I really am, and to my brother-in-law Joe Aakre who has bailed me out of more computer snafoos than I care to mention. It is difficult to find words to express how thankful I am for your expressions of love to me, but especially for how much you loved Mo. You flew her across the country with you on an all-expense paid vacation, just so you could show her how special she was; she knew she was loved because of you.

To Michael Bingham, for being the big brother she was inspired by and looked up to. For making it a point to include her in your world by taking her shopping downtown whenever you'd visit, like you were showing off your little sister. She felt cool because of you.

To Sarah Bingham, her big sister, for teaching her about girly stuff like makeup, but also the importance of being well-read: you were teaching her to be proud of herself... and for writing her letters that tried to take the pain away. She felt understood because of you.

Praise for *Once the Storm is Over*

"Author Nina Bingham doesn't avoid the hard parts in recounting a riveting and painfully honest account of life before and after the death of her daughter to suicide. *Once the Storm is Over* offers readers of all persuasions a rare glimpse of the human condition with heartfelt words of courage, change, and comfort."
~Rita Robinson, *Survivors of Suicide*

"Gripping, bold and progressive-the gutsiest new autobiography on grief I've seen in years. An emerging writer we must hear more from."
~ Kathleen Sanderfer, *Mom, I'm Alright*

"Raw, honest, powerful and inspiring, *Once The Storm Is Over* takes us through the authors personal struggle with depression, and how she manages to survive the loss of her beloved daughter Moriyah to the same demons she herself fought her entire life. Once the storm settles, Nina picks up the pieces of her life and honors her daughter's memory by having the courage to share her story in hopes of helping others. A must-read for anyone who has suffered a loss due to suicide."
~ Magdaline DeSousa, *The Forgotten Mourners: Sibling Survivors of Suicide*

"Nina Bingham rips apart the façade of coping to show the devastating aftermath of a child's suicide and how a mother, flawed but courageous, learns to live again. This important contribution to the literature of suicide is told with strong passion and authenticity that shakes the reader, allowing us to share her experience."
~ Marion Crook, *Out of the Darkness: Teens Talk About Suicide*, and *Every Parent's Guide to Understanding Teenagers and Suicide: Recognize the Hidden Signs*

"Nina bears her soul: her guilt, her love, and her acceptance of all the pain. Read this book-and be immersed in grace."
~ Vanessa Bednar, *Left Behind: My Suicide Survivor Story: Releasing Guilt and Finding Joy After a Loved Ones Suicide*

"I had to search for the right word to describe this book—'powerful' does not do justice to either the story or the author. 'Shattering' and 'healing' apply, but even they fall short. One word truly fits, however: 'important.' Despite Nina's wonderful writing style, *Once the Storm is Over* is an emotional read. But books about this topic should be difficult, particularly for those of us who have had our own struggles. To have an impact, books about sensitive topics like mental illness and suicide need to be genuine and caring, but they also need to be brutally honest. This is one of the few books about mental illness that manages to be both. An amazing book of both suffering and triumph."

~ Sean Bennick, *Mental Health Matters*

"This book is a worthy reference for understanding suicide because of its profound insight on a very personal level. For an issue that is extremely hard to talk about, Nina does so with candidness that is both courageous and admirable. I've encountered those who wish to depict suicide as a rational act, or who disparage themselves for not observing the signs. This book provides much clarity on both views."

~ Joan Treppa, Citizen Advocate for the Minnesota Innocence Project

"A brave, insightful, and enlightened read... powerful and touching, a story that transcends the suicide of her daughter, and one that will aid all those who grieve the untimely loss of a loved one."

~John J. Higgins, *The Archangel Jarahmael* and *The War to Conquer Heaven Series*, and host of *Hanging With Higgins Radio Show*

"Every year in the United States there are over 30,000 suicides; that is more than the population of the town I live in. Nina does a great job of bringing forward all of the emotions of a suicide survivor, and explains feelings that people don't want to, or can't talk about. *Once The Storm Is Over* is the beginning of the healing process."

~ Bill MacPhee, Magpie Media and *Mental Wellness Today Magazine*

"As a professional, Nina Bingham was trained to spot the signs of danger, but as a mother, she was afraid to push too hard; afraid to alienate her troubled daughter with endless questions about how she felt and whether she was taking her meds. *Once the Storm is Over* is Nina's journey through grief and devastating guilt to a place of not just acceptance, but powerful gratitude and grace. This amazing book will be of immeasurable help to anyone trying to recover from the suicide of a loved one."

~ Sandra Champlain, *We Don't Die: A Skeptics View of the Afterlife* and host of *We Don't Die Radio Show*

"Experiencing the loss of a child is undoubtedly one of the most painful and difficult experiences. Not only does Nina Bingham share with us her daughters suicide, and how she learned to cope with it, but she also lays bare the painful path that led to it. Growing up with an abusive alcoholic father, failed marriage, suffering the rejection of coming out as a lesbian, and her own brush with suicide. What could have been a story mired in self pity and misery, ultimately is a story of hope. Nina's compelling life journey shows how pain and loss can be transformed into strength and purpose. This book is not only for survivors but for anyone facing depression with suicidal tendencies. Five stars."

~ Ralph Smith, *Seal of the King*

"Nina Bingham's book is a jolt to the heart to any of us who have survived suicide or raised children in the shadow of it. As Nina says, so many parents cannot imagine surviving the death of their child, and neither could she, but she does! She chooses health and healing and light despite being driven to her knees, heartbroken by her daughter's suicide. This anguished love story will haunt you and inspire you. I ask you to read it. For your sake."

~ Dr. David Treadway, *Dead Reckoning: A Therapist Confronts His Own Grief*

"Tragedy happens in families whether you are a gay or straight parent. In her memoir, *Once The Storm Is Over*, Nina Bingham offers valuable insight to others by sharing her experience of generational clinical depression, coming out in a religious family, and of her daughter's suicide. A gifted writer, Bingham is also a courageous soul."
~ Angeline Acain, *Gay Parents Magazine*

"In this unflinching memoir, Nina Bingham shares her unique grief journey after the death of her precious daughter. Nina's story courageously lays out these truths: Grief's hurt is essential, and expressing it even more essential. If you do the hard work of grief, you will find grace, hope, and healing. And true love…well, true love never dies."
~ Dr. Alan D. Wolfelt, Director of the Center for Loss and Life Transition, and author of *Understanding Your Grief: Ten Essential Touchstones for Finding Hope and Healing Your Heart*, and the *Healing Your Grieving Heart Series*

"Unabashedly honest in her evaluation of self and others, Ms. Bingham invites you into her personal world following her daughter's unexpected suicide. Every parent navigating the hurdles following such a tragic loss needs to read *Once The Storm is Over* for a brilliantly lit roadmap to hope, understanding and forgiveness."
~ Marlayna Glynn Brown, *The Scattering of All: Tales From Extraordinary Survivors of Suicide Loss*

"Nina Bingham's raw and honest sharing of her own journey following her daughter's suicide navigates the familiar questions: Why couldn't I have prevented this? What more should I have done? Her unflinching story reaffirms the transformative power of grief and offers the hope that after devastation comes healing and renewal."
~ Judith Galas, *The Power to Prevent Suicide: A Guide for Teens Helping Teens*

"*Once the Storm is Over* is a raw, real read-but one which is ultimately filled with grace and forgiveness. To expose your most vulnerable self to the world; the good, the not so good, and the tragic, is brave and beautiful. Nina's story is uniquely her own, yet so relatable. I found myself entirely entwined in her feelings by a tie that binds many of us—that of suicide. Yet ultimately, I felt the tie that binds *all* of us—that of love."

~ Leslie Stickel, speaker and author of *Hope Defined: Learning to Live With The Loss of a Loved One*

"Most of us think we know how much pressured devastation our hearts can endure before coming out the other side brighter and more colossal. But Nina Bingham presents grief as a multifaceted stone to hold up to a new light: her unique story, and its profound truth. *Once the Storm Is Over* provides the honest details of enormous loss, and the many angles of heartbreak which the human psyche can endure."

~ Carrie Seitzinger, *NAILED Magazine*

For Moriyah,
who taught me everything I needed to know
about life, and death.

"And once the storm is over, you won't remember how you made it through, how you managed to survive. You won't even be sure, whether the storm is really over. But one thing is certain. When you come out of the storm, you won't be the same person who walked in. That's what this storm's all about."

~ Haruki Murakami

INTRODUCTION

Back in 2012, Nina approached me with an idea for a book she was writing based on knowledge gained from her years as a Life Coach. The writing was solid and so was the advice, but as I told her, I found myself wishing there was more about the author; that the presentation was more intimate, and had a stronger sense of us knowing who is telling us these things. She responded promptly that she felt the same way, and was going to "sit on the manuscript" for awhile. What impresses an editor most is when a writer accepts feedback with grace, and I knew then that Nina was someone I wanted to be friends with— and I knew that at some point we would work together.

We started hanging out on Facebook. Her posts were wise, funny, powerful and inspiring. While I was taking care of my parents who were both dying, her comments were full of love, encouragement, and sympathy.

Then came from her the shocking announcement that her daughter had committed suicide. How in the world do you respond to that? My heart shattered for her; I PMd her, told her how sorry I was, asked if there was anything I could do. When she replied, I was amazed at how calm she was. She was almost peaceful. She seemed focused on the fact that her daughter's pain was now over. I sat in awe of her.

I kept checking in, and watched her strength unfold. She didn't seem angry or bitter. She had achieved a sort of Divine Acceptance that I just couldn't imagine being possible.

About six months later she approached me again, this time with the story of how she really dealt with her daughter's suicide; the real story, not the brave façade she'd put up for us all, and as I read the manuscript, my heart broke again. I was honored to have been the one she contacted.

Now it's my turn to be honest—I sat and read her manuscript in one sitting, and knew that she had a blockbuster story. As a publisher, I was drawn to the sheer commercial appeal—the great characters, the poignancy, the relevant topic, the thematic movement of her journey.

As her friend, however, I wanted what was best for her. Big Table Publishing is a small indie press, and I felt that Nina had the kind of story that a big house would want. I wrestled with my conscience all day, and that evening, I sat down and sent her an e-mail saying how much I loved the story, but that I thought she should get an agent and sell it to a big place like Random House or something; a place that could spend thousands of dollars promoting it, maybe send her on a book tour.

To my surprise, she wrote back and said, no, she specifically wanted Big Table Publishing to do the book. As it turned out, she'd gone to a psychic and had mentioned that she was writing a book about her daughter's suicide. When she asked the psychic about getting a publisher, the psychic said, "I see a woman, she has a literary community around her. You already know this person. She is nice, and you can trust her. She will do what is in your best interest. Don't be afraid to go with her, she will help you get where you need to go."

Nina's e-mail went on, "Of course when she said it I knew instantly it was you, I mean how much clearer could it have been? That's why when you suggested I go to a larger house, I chuckled. You're the only publisher I know, and you fit that description. So here we are."

So here we are, indeed!

Working with Nina has been a pleasure beyond words. Her courage, her wisdom, her incredible transformation, in addition to her superior writing skills, truly made this the dream project. And as Nina would say, we're all just ghosts in each other's dreams, anyway!

Robin Stratton, January 2015
Boston, MA

PROLOGUE

I HUNG UP THE PHONE, frustrated. "Sons of bitches," I said.

"What's wrong?" asked Rachael, my fiancée.

"They said that Mo's therapy isn't covered by my insurance!"

"How can that be? I thought you said it was."

"I thought it was… but it's not." I dropped onto the couch. "So what do I do, sit back and watch my daughter sink deeper and deeper?"

Rachael sat next to me, her eyes on my face so that she could read my lips. Deaf since she was two years old, she was not given to empty conversation; now, however, she obviously couldn't come up with anything to say.

"That's the problem with insurance companies," I said. "You can't fight them. They're too big."

Rachael sighed. We'd had this conversation before–several times I'd been told *No* when it came to financing treatment for my daughter's depression.

I sighed too. Maybe it didn't even matter. *She sat the whole time and didn't say a word*, was what therapists in the past had told me. As a life coach, I knew the process of getting a client to communicate was tricky. You had to know what questions to ask, you couldn't sound like you were grilling them, and even if you figured out their issue in the first five minutes, you had to let them come to it when they were ready, it had to be their personal discovery. Moriyah had been so stubborn about going. For the billionth time, I sat back; felt responsible. Depression was nothing new to me. In fact, the depression gene running rampant in my family was probably the reason I'd gone into the field of psychology in the first place.

"We have to do *something*," Rachael said. "What would you suggest if this was one of your clients?"

"Well… sometimes bargaining works. You tell them that unless they stop a certain behavior, you're going to take them to a hospital."

Rachael grimaced. "She would hate that. Could you really do it?"

"I'd have to. That would have to be the deal. It couldn't be an empty threat."

"Maybe the anti-depressants will do the job," Rachael said. "You told me they don't always work right away. Maybe just give her a little time."

"Maybe. I actually think she's been a tiny bit better, don't you?"

Rachael nodded. "I didn't want to say anything, but yeah, I feel like she's been less depressed. She's a little more chatty."

"Oh thank God, I thought I was imagining it!"

"I thought I was!"

"So the meds must be working! Okay, so we'll just have faith that she'll be okay."

After a few weeks we began to see appreciable changes in Mo's mood. It was thrilling to see her beautiful smile again, like the sun coming out after a horrible winter. She began eating dinner with us again, and discussing activities at school. Her grades went back up, and she joined her school's local chapter of The Red Cross, which meant weekly club meetings and baking cookies to raise money for disaster relief funds. When she was voted the club's representative, I thought I would cry; I was so proud, and so relieved.

"Let's watch a movie together," Mo suggested one night.

"Okay!" I couldn't keep the joy out of my voice.

"How about this?" she asked, holding up *Madea's Family Reunion*.

"I know you love it."

So there we sat, my daughter, her new puppy Romeo, my fiancée, and me, watching one of my favorite movies. I had a great time hooting and hollering, clapping my hands in delight. I could feel Moriyah smiling. She told me once that her favorite thing about me was my infectious laugh. After the movie, she said she was going to bed.

"Love you," I said, and then kissed the top of Romeo's head as he dozed in her arms. "And him."

"I'm so glad you and Rachael are engaged," she said suddenly, "so I won't have to worry about you." She smiled with a serenity that made me happy. For years I'd worried about her–that she was depressed, that she was never going to be well, that she would harm herself–but that night I didn't; I slept soundly.

CHAPTER ONE

SOME OF MY EARLIEST MEMORIES are of my Grandma Bea cooking up a storm for Mardi Gras: a humble, portly lady, she heaped our plates with black-eyed peas, cornbread and fried okra. She boiled dimes in the beans, and a doll head was hidden in the King's Cake. *The more dimes you get in your bowl of beans, the luckier your year will be! It's a Mardi Gras tradition!* she'd say. I never understood why Mardi Gras was such a big deal, because we lived in California. When she wasn't cooking, she was worrying. Pacing, muttering, wringing her hands. Or lying in bed crying for reasons I couldn't understand. It seemed as if she was fine one day, then so sad the next. Sometimes she would go to a place my father called a "sanitarium," and when we visited, I hated the morbid silence and stale hopelessness pervading the large sterile rooms. Residents were doped-up and slumped over in wheelchairs, or aimlessly wandering the halls like zombies, while orderlies and nurses walked around in white shoes, looking at papers on clip boards. When I got older, I was told the reason Grandma Bea had to go to the hospital was because she had threatened to kill herself. "She's going to have electroshock therapy treatments," my father told me, "and that will make her better." But it didn't. When she came home she was subdued, uncommunicative, and she drooled, her jaw shifting oddly to one side. When she did speak, she slurred her words. She never cooked again.

Before I started going to school my mother stayed home, and my father was a blue-collar tradesman. Early pictures of us show a happy, cohesive family with a sleek new car and middle-class suburban home. When my father was sober, he was a charming and clever man who would regale us with humorous tales. But diagnosed with what they used to call Manic Depressive Disorder, he refused medication, and was an abusive alcoholic; a violent, raging sadist. He used male privilege to control, treating my mother like his servant, and espousing white supremacist rhetoric. He used intimidation and blame to "normalize" the abuse. His psychological tactics were effective; we all kept the family secret.

My mother received the lion's share of my father's wrath. One time he broke her hand; another time he shoved her down the stairs. This was her reward for working 12 hours a day at her beauty salon– managing a small business and keeping our family afloat while he stayed drunk and unemployed.

Being alone in our three-story house with my father was like being trapped in a big haunted house with the devil. I often hid in the crawlspaces of my house so I could feel safe; he was too burly to get in. One time, when I was 10, and just starting to "develop," he came into the bathroom when I was in the shower. He was drunk. I opened the shower curtain and saw him in the doorway, leering. I'd seen that look on his face a million times, that look that said he was coming after me. I started screaming at the top of my lungs. He told me to shut up, and left in a hurry. My father's cruelty and lack of love and attention drove me to conclude that I was worthless and stupid.

My home was a volatile and terrifying place. My parents fought vigorously and in front of my brother and sister and me. I remember my father's drunken threats growing louder and more frightening with each drink. When I counted the empty beer cans and gallon bottles of cheap wine, I would wonder how he could consume so much and still stand upright.

The nightly arguments interfered with my school work, and one evening my mother sat me on the couch and gently delivered the news that I wouldn't be going on to the second grade like the rest of my friends. *I'm stupid!* I realized; *Maybe I'm retarded!* In the 1970s nobody ever inquired if I was struggling to learn due to my turbulent home life, and my mother, steeped in her own shame, never explained the situation to my teachers. So I stayed behind, and when I started first grade over again, I tried to blend in, but I was a year older, and I was taller than the other kids. When they asked me how old I was, I'd tell them I was a year younger. Even though they seemed like babies to me, I was afraid they'd judge me for having stayed back a year.

When I was ten my parents separated with the approval of my mother's church. My father was told he would have to submit to a process by which they would start from scratch to mend the relationship. My mother was being "discipled" by a man at her Bible college, and was expected to follow his rules and guidance. Her "discipler" decided that my dad would have to learn respect again for his wife, and that meant living separately, and beginning the slow process of dating again. I remember my mother being thrilled when my father, trying to go along with it to save the marriage, brought her a rose on one of their first dates. But I knew his temper, and I knew this contrived format was doomed to fail. My mother wanted to mold him into a proper Christian husband, and that wasn't going to happen. Sure enough, she finally realized that he wasn't willing to be "discipled." In a weird way, I was glad. Even though I feared my dad and didn't want him back home, I couldn't stand the thought of a religious know-it-all telling my dad what to do. It made me think of stories I'd read of crazy wild stallions having their spirits broken so they could be ridden by cowboys.

23

I had a younger sister, Rhonda, and a younger brother, David, and my father made an effort to stick around for us, for a while. He rented a shabby, broken-down apartment on the wrong side of town. His small TV had rabbit ears and sat on a tray table next to his never-made bed, and in his tiny kitchen dirty dishes filled the sink and covered the counters and the stove. We could smell the dumpster from the doorway, and our playground became the abandoned shopping carts left in the parking lot. His apartment was so dirty and dismal that I dreaded our weekends with him. I would hide in the house when he came to pick us up, and my mother would have to coax me into his beat-up pickup truck. One time while he was putting gas in the truck I opened his glove box to snoop, and found a box of rubbers. Why would he need them if he still loved my mother? Disgusted, I put them back, buried under a bunch of papers so my sister and brother wouldn't find them. Our visits stopped after a girl who lived in his complex, not much older than me, tried to shiv me in the parking lot. One minute we were playing, and the next she grabbed me by the shirt and brandished a knife. I wriggled out of her grasp and ran for my life. I told my father what had happened and he reported it to the complex manager. After that, he didn't come to pick us up anymore, he just called once a week. I dreaded his calls, too, because he always cried when it was time to say goodbye.

When I was eleven my mother decided it was time for a divorce. My father reacted by threatening to kill her. She told her parents, and a few days later they pulled up to the house in their big green car (a source of embarrassment to us kids—we called it "the Hearse") and told us to get in. They'd brought coolers with bologna and cheese sandwiches on wheat bread, tents, sleeping bags and the Hibachi BBQ, and we headed to the ocean for the summer. We kids were excited, but my mother walked the beach weeping and trying to figure how she was going to put together the shattered pieces of her life. When Fall came, she registered us at the school in my grandparents' town. My father showed up waving a shotgun. My brother and sister and I hid in my Grandpa's shop behind the house, trying to stay calm as we ate chicken and donuts. *Like Anne Frank*, I thought, having just finished reading her diary.

Meanwhile, my mother's mother, a sturdy, stalwart woman who lived through the Great Depression and who at 12 was left to care for her two younger brothers when her mother died of cancer, had a nononsense approach that somehow got through to my dad. He retreated, and eventually moved. We were able to return to our house and our school. My father, we were told, moved away; but not without leaving a gift for each of us kids; for me, an album by Seals & Crofts. I was so surprised that he knew how much I liked them. For a moment, I felt… perhaps loved by him.

As a child I had innocently admired his energy, swagger and bravado. It had been hard to understand how such a hero of a man could turn into someone who would slam my mother's fingers repeatedly in the door, or whip us kids with his belt. As his illness escalated, he would make us "dinners" by grinding up God-knows what in a blender and commanding us to gag down disgusting pink and brown concoctions, roaring with laughter at our tears. One day he said if I could run up the stairs to my room before he could catch me, I'd be spared a beating. I remember his maniacal laugh as he bounded up the stairs hot on my heels. As fast as I could, I ran into the unfinished cubby hole–safe because he was too big to fit in. I realized how truly pathetic he was the afternoon he came home so drunk that he began to weep, confessing his impotence as a father and husband to me, and pissed his pants right in front of me. I was about 10 years old, but I remember being terribly embarrassed for him. I helped him to his bedroom so he could change and I never told my mother or anyone about the humiliating scene.

When I was in the fourth grade my mother sold the family piano and bought me a ukulele. "Learn three songs on this," she said, handing me sheet music, "and I'll buy you a guitar." I learned

25

to play that ukulele as quick as a flash! From then on it was a love affair between my guitar and me. I wrote music prolifically, blotting out my home life by immersing myself in music.

One day at school the other students and I were working quietly at our desks when all of a sudden our teacher, Miss Anderson, started shrieking at the top of her lungs, and then she ran head-long into the sliding glass door. There was a *CRASH* and glass everywhere, and then Miss Anderson lay on the floor whimpering and bleeding. We all just sat in shock, staring at her; only a moment ago, she'd been fine! The teacher in the next classroom must have heard the commotion, because within just a few moments adults flooded the room. We were herded outside, confused and frightened. An ambulance arrived and Miss Andersen was carted away on a stretcher. We were told she "wasn't well" and needed to go to the hospital. I was shocked that even a teacher could be mentally ill.

I was never held back again, but the sense that I was stupid created a major inferiority complex, and as I began each year I always assumed I'd be too stupid to pass. My high school math teacher, Mr. Dice, did nothing to assuage my doubts. A balding old jock and the school's beloved football coach, he was a crabby sexist who liked to make girls feel dumb if they asked questions. We all quickly learned to keep our mouths shut as he announced that while girls excelled in English and home economics, it was a proven fact that boys were better in math and science. The "important" topics. He said the best we girls could hope for was to pass the class with a C. And in fact, I got a C-.

Despite the fact that my father told my mother he wanted no contact with his kids, and then started moving a lot to avoid paying child support, at the age of 16 I decided to visit him for the summer. I was hoping that he had changed; I yearned for a normal father-daughter relationship. So I went to see him in his trailer home in the middle of a dusty orange grove in Visalia. By the front door, spindly near-dead flowers sprouted from an old cracked toilet; inside, it was dim and gloomy. To my disappointment, nothing had changed–he still got drunk every single night. For a whole summer he ranted maniacally about the government, and how the country was going to pot because of all the minorities (but he didn't say "minorities," he used another word), getting up to piss outside his backdoor instead of in the bathroom.

The highlight of the visit was the date my father arranged for me with a boy who was an usher at his conservative Christian church; Roy was a handsome, quiet boy. He took me to see *Caddy Shack*, but he wasn't interested in the movie. As soon as the lights went out, he put his hands in my underwear. Sexually naive and still a virgin, I sat in my seat, rigid with panic. I wanted to bolt, but was afraid that my father would be mad. Besides, how would I get home? So I just shut my eyes and endured his fumbling. When the movie ended he suggested we go for a drive, but I told him I had to get home. I let myself into the trailer, and my father, sitting in the living room watching television, asked if I'd had a nice time. I didn't even answer, I just went straight to the bathroom, scrubbed myself in the shower, and cried. Only then did I admit to myself that going there had been a huge mistake.

Two years later I met the man I would marry. We were both members of a church youth group that espoused conventional views of religion. We married when I was 23, and my mission in life was mapped out for me: to be the perfect wife and mother.

I tried, I really did. Homemade bread and pies made from scratch with apples from our tree. A hot dinner on the table every night. The house sparkling clean; the yard, too. In 1987 I gave birth to our son Michael; a daughter, Sarah, followed in 1989. As a dutiful stay-at-home mom, I took in the neighborhood "strays" (latchkey kids) to show my Christian charity. I did my best to ignore my husband's porn addiction (which I discovered three weeks into the marriage) and when we moved to Oregon and he got fired for looking at porn at work, I got us by on a shoestring budget. There were several online affairs, and one summer he took our vacation money and flew out of state to meet someone he'd met in a chat room (she turned out to be too fat for his liking.) Finally, after nine years, two separations, and a failed attempt at counseling, I called it quits.

I had also met someone else. My boss. My married boss. And for the trifecta of complications, my married boss was a woman.

For as long as I could remember, I'd had crushes on girls or my female teachers, and when I was 18 I was in love with my best friend. We used to cuddle, but never allowed our actions to get sexual, because we'd been taught it was a sin. But now, at last, here I was, a full-grown woman head over heels with another full-grown woman whose husband neglected and ignored her. During our first business trip together, we abandoned ourselves to our emotions, and something inside me unlocked; I realized that this was what I needed, the emotional intimacy I had not been able to get from my husband or any of my boyfriends. After a couple of months I told her I was leaving my husband, but she said she couldn't leave hers. So we parted ways—I was unhappy, but relieved. At last I knew what was "wrong" with me when it came to men.

But the Church teachings still had a hold on me, and I decided I would give men one more chance. Soon I was dating Eddie Jones, the most decent person I had ever met; kind, stable, successful, and gentle. And boring—to me, at least. We dated for the longest six months of my life, and in that time, I could only bring myself to have sex with him twice. But apparently twice, even while using birth control, was enough, because I got pregnant with Moriyah. This is why I have always believed that I was meant to have her.

As soon as I found out I was going to have a baby, I decided to be honest with Eddie. I knew he was going to insist we do the "right thing" and get married (he had already proposed twice and I had already said No twice), and I knew that would never work. So I told him that I would always love him, that I wanted him to be in our daughter's life, but that I would be raising her on my own. He agreed, not just because he was a sweet, wonderful man, but because he had no choice.

Once I came out to Eddie, I also broke out of the strict holding pattern my life had been in. I'd become what my family, husband and church expected me to be: self-sacrificing and submissive. It was time to realize my own identity.

Instead of meeting with my mother and step-father, I sent them a letter. My mother's second husband had a degree from a conservative Christian school of theology, and a long history of being a board member in churches. His passion was teaching Bible studies in their home. My mother had attended Bible school and was the proverbial pastor's wife; in fact, congregants called her the "church mom." No matter how I broke the news to them, I was pretty sure it would be the end of our relationship. So I sent the letter and held my breath. I didn't hear back from them for weeks. No phone calls, no emails. It was like waiting for a bomb to land. Finally I received two letters, one from each of them. Mom's letter was heartfelt: *Where did I go wrong?* She said she was disappointed in me, and that I had let her down. My stepfather's letter was a rambling six-page Biblical indictment of my homosexuality in which he threatened that unless I turned back, I would go to hell. He signed it *Pastor Greg*. I felt sick and disowned: this was a man I'd come to trust and think of as my father. I made a fire and watched his letter burn. To my mother's credit, she met with another older woman in their church whose child had also come out, in an attempt to understand gay culture: "She told me all about gay sex and how deviant it is. She told me there were leather bars and M&M clubs. You're not involved in anything dangerous, are you?" I wanted to joke, "I don't belong to any M&M clubs, but believe me, if I could find one I would join, I love M&Ms!" I just chuckled and put my arm around her worried stooped shoulders. "It's S&M,

Mom, and no, I don't do any of that stuff. I haven't even been dating that much." I told her I was glad we were talking about it, and that she could always ask me anything about my lifestyle. But she shook her head. "From here on out, I don't want to know anything at all about it. If you bring someone over, I don't want you to have any physical contact when you're in my house. I don't want you to talk about this ever again."

It was a major blow. All my life I'd admired her unwavering service to a concept she believed in. But like so many church goers, her judgment was harsh and unwavering.

Even worse was my meeting with the pastor. I'd donated hundreds of volunteer hours to his church (not to mention dollars), and felt we owed it to each other to have an adult conversation about this. He welcomed me into his office, told me to have a seat, and asked me to explain why I was divorcing my husband. I shared what nine years of living with an addict had been like, and he agreed my grounds were justified. "Also," I said hesitantly, "I, uh, I've fallen in love. With a woman." His eye brows shot to the ceiling. I kept going. "For the first time in my life, I feel happy. And I don't want to hide this, I want to be honest about it."

He glared; his shoulders were hunched as if fending off an attack of evil. "Nina, you're welcome to attend services here, but you're not allowed to sing in the choir or lead worship at women's Bible studies or retreats. You're not allowed to hold any position at all in *my* church."

"I see." I stood.

He held out his hand and said coldly, "Good luck."

I felt as if I'd been tossed out with the trash. I turned and left without shaking his hand. Why had I thought I could have an honest conversation with this man? He clearly wasn't interested in discussing anything. So just like that, I'd been disinherited by my parents and my church. But at least I'd been honest with myself. I walked out with tears burning in my eyes, but my head held high; a little taller than when I'd walked in.

CHAPTER TWO

LIKE A PRISONER RELEASED I walked into a new world; a world of freedom and unlimited possibilities. It was overwhelming, intimidating, exciting. I returned to college to complete my degree in Psychology. I dated and explored my sexuality with women. I was like a sponge soaking up all the freewheeling fun I'd previously denied myself. My best coming-out memory is the first time I ever visited a lesbian bar. It took me weeks of thinking it over but I finally got up the courage. I went by myself because I didn't know any other gay people, and I was so shy that I refused every dance. A wallflower, I sipped my drink with a lump in my throat and a nervous knot in my stomach, peeking discreetly over the top of my glass as butch and femme women paired off throughout the night. *You're going to hell in a hand basket*, I muttered to myself... *any minute the devil's ganna come walking right through that door!* My heart thudded so hard I thought it was going to pop out of my shirt. At the same time, I felt so happy to see other women who liked women. And so many different kinds of women! From the soccer moms (who probably drove their mini vans to the bar) and high-class business types in crisp business suits and heels, to toothless women who looked like they'd just fallen out of their trailers, and computer nerds with thick glasses and pencils in their button down shirt pockets. There were fast talkers and shy head duckers (like me).

There was a bouquet of color in the room–white, black, brown… a smorgasbord of lesbian goodness. I remember wanting to shout, "I've found my people!"

I began to investigate other things I'd been told by the church to stay away from; every witchy, voodoo, heebie jeebie activity the church feared. I underwent hypnosis to give up smoking, and then enrolled and graduated from a clinical hypnotherapy program. Fascinated by the intuitive energy work of Reiki, I took courses and became a certified Reiki Master. I set up a private practice in an integrated medical clinic, working alongside non-traditional physicians, naturopaths, chiropractors, massage therapists, and acupuncturists. This was a world that welcomed–even celebrated– departures from the "norm." A world that accepted and embraced.

I was finally living an authentic life, but my divorce was a financial disaster. I was a single mother with two children, working full-time and traveling for my job, and frequently taking courses. I was awarded the house and full custody, but I couldn't afford to pay the mortgage on one meager salary, so I had to sell. By the time all the attorney bills were paid, all I put in the bank was $500.

Further complicating the situation was the fact that my son was hyperactive and having difficulty in school. He was now eleven, and had started asking me questions that a father should be answering. I asked my ex if he would take our son, and he agreed. Their relationship had been rocky when we all lived together, but had gotten smoother once my ex moved out. My son seemed to respect and obey his father, and I felt that he would be better off there. My daughter missed her brother terribly, and eventually said she'd like to go live with her dad too. My heart broke. I knew if she left she'd never come back. But it was what she wanted, so I said Yes. Almost immediately my ex announced that he was taking the kids away from Oregon to go back to California. The kids were delighted because they loved their California grandparents and hated the Oregon rain, but I cried for weeks. I couldn't stand the thought of losing them. But his parents could give him the new start he needed, and were affluent enough to offer my kids the opportunities that a single mom living on food stamps couldn't. I told myself I was being a good parent, doing what was best for my children, not myself... still, I felt like a colossal failure.

I buried myself in my new personal and professional identity, but my genetic propensity for mental illness went into high gear and I was swamped by intense, unrelenting depression. My dream of becoming a therapist was slipping from my grasp, thwarted by my own psychological issues. I slept like the dead, but woke each morning exhausted, and my body felt like lead. I stopped going to class. I stopped going to work (I was a psychiatric technician). Nothing mattered to me except sleep. Forget doing housework— even the act of picking up the phone was overwhelming to me. So there I was, studying mental illness with the goal of becoming a therapist, and at the same time, was caught in the grip of the very hopelessness and helplessness that I was studying! I couldn't bear to tell my professors or co-workers or boss why I wasn't able to attend class anymore; just the thought of explaining exhausted me. I didn't even have the energy to cry. Sleep was the only escape from this pain, which of course was my family's curse. My other option was suicide, and I thought about it whenever I was awake. This went on for almost three years, costing me my job, my studies, my apartment and my car. The only thing I really cared about was Moriyah, and every day I would wait in my empty room in my parents' attic for her to get home from school. I existed only when she was with me. When she was gone, so was I.

I was so incapacitated that I was unable to speak my mind even in the company of family and friends. I would sit miserably on the sidelines of conversation, a silent observer. My personality had always been exuberant and talkative. Where had that bubbly girl gone? The only thing that seemed to distract me from the negative thoughts and feelings was reading. When I was reading I was transported to another world where mental illness didn't exist, and during those three horrible years, I read 150 books, mostly about world religion, metaphysics, spirituality and psychology. The scientific term for this is "bibliotherapy" and even though I don't think I realized it then, I was using reading not just to educate myself, but to rewire my brain to prepare for healing.

One day a friend called, and as soon as she heard my voice, she said, "I'm coming over." She was at my door in less than ten minutes; dressed me, and whisked me away to my physician's office. My doctor took one look at me, and said, "I've never seen you like this."

I hung my head and accepted the judgment in silence and shame.

"Nina," she said gently, "this is not your fault. This is a medical diagnosis, you know that."

"I know, but…"

"We're going to get you on a couple of anti-depressants, and in less than a month, you'll be back to your old self again."

As she wrote up the prescriptions, hope trickled in. Maybe she was right, maybe I'd be okay. So I started taking medication, and within a couple of weeks, my energy level returned and the storm clouds began to lift. Soon the thought of suicide seemed ridiculous. What was I thinking?

Each day I felt a little surer and a little stronger in my conviction that I would come out the other side of what had felt like a long black tunnel. I began to see that maybe some good could come of it; maybe my experience could benefit someone else. Armed with real-life experience with how it felt to suffer with mental illness, I resumed my college classes (my professors extended my course work deadlines) and at last, my mental health stabilized.

I met someone new, and we were married in Oregon in 2004. A year later, Oregon overturned the same-sex marriage law, and suddenly we weren't married anymore. We moved to Arizona, and for the next three years I struggled to manage symptoms of low-grade depression. While the anti-depressants got me out of bed and kept me reasonably productive, anxiety stood resolutely between me and happiness. Eventually I couldn't relate sexually to my girlfriend; I started telling her that I needed to go home to be with family. I was irritable, overly serious, and socially anxious. Not surprisingly, her affections strayed.

Though devastated and betrayed, part of me understood.

Once again I had to own up to failure caused by my mental illness. It was summer, and Mo was staying with her father, and I longed to see her again. So I packed up and took a cab to the airport to go home.

As I waited to board the plane, it suddenly hit me that I wasn't feeling depressed or anxious. Some calm voice–the Inner Me or the Universe? Does it matter?–whispered, "You can throw away the medicine now; you're not going to need it anymore."

Now this was truly crazy. Those pills were the only thing keeping me sane; indeed, keeping me alive. But for reasons I can't explain, I felt certain that the symptoms were gone for good. I found a trash receptacle and tossed the bottle of pills in without a moment's hesitation. "Don't worry," said the voice. And then I saw myself, like watching a movie: My whole life I'd been unhappy, but had forced myself to be what others wanted me to be: a good daughter, a good wife, a good mother, a good partner. Denying what I wanted for *my* life created conflict and anxiety. So I denied being unhappy, and in that way, attempted to suppress pain. Suppressing the pain made it impossible to see the pain, or acknowledge and treat it.

Once I understood this, I was filled with a feeling I had not known: it was peace. I felt myself giggle. I got on the plane, dazed by the revelation, and as I settled myself and looked out the window, I heard the voice say, "You are the creator of your life. You are the architect of your own life."

CHAPTER THREE

IF AN OUTSIDER were to describe my love life, they might say I was one relationship away from being a country song. My first serious relationship lasted five years; the second and third just a year. The fourth, my same-sex marriage, lasted four years. It seemed that Mo and I were always on the move, which meant she had to change schools multiple times. Over the years this instability caused her to withdraw further and further into her own world. Already an innately quiet and sensitive child, she spoke very little, preferring to say everything with her big brown doe-eyes. She loved to draw, and spent endless hours in her room. But all she ever drew was a picture of a girl; a girl always alone. With each woman that passed through my life, she allowed herself to care less and less. Each time she had to say goodbye, my heart broke for her.

But as women wove in and out of our lives, one thing remained constant: our mother-daughter bond. Because of the losses, we clung to one another all the more. After each breakup, I'd hold her and feel like that old song, "You and Me Against the World." I'd spend all my free time with her–holding her, teaching her to read, coloring with her, singing her to sleep, laughing at silly cartoons, cooking with her, being her audience as she played at the park. I even squeezed myself into her small bed every night until she fell asleep. But in the mornings when she left for school I'd hold back the tears until she was out of sight. I was so scared that something bad would happen while we were apart.

If I could have kept her with me every minute, I would have. This desperate feeling of needing to be with her stretched even into junior high, and when she began, appropriately, to grow away from me as pre-teens do, the uneasy feeling of needing to be with her got worse.

One morning I was soaking in the bathtub, severely depressed, sobbing out my torment. I had written a suicide letter earlier that week, and I was prepared to go. I had orchestrated it all very carefully: a friend was coming over, and she would discover my body, not Mo. And no one would have to clean up a mess, because I was in the bathtub. All of a sudden from the other room Mo began screaming, "Mommy, Mommy!" She was a quiet child who never raised her voice... why now? All I wanted to do was to die! But I couldn't just let her stand out there and scream. What if something was wrong? Immediately I realized the irony of the situation—my suicide would be the ultimate injury, and would scar her forever. So with tears running down my face, I dragged my body out of the tub, dried off, and went out to be with her. She literally saved my life that day.

Then I met and fell in love with Rachael, and in her gentle, trustworthy way, she completed our family; there we were, two newly-engaged middle-aged lesbians raising a teen daughter—what they call an "emerging family."

Mo adored Rachael, and seeing me happy took a lot of pressure off her. Sometimes she'd wanted to stay with her father, but had felt obligated to stay with me. Now she didn't have to.

Because of my ever-changing love life, Mo idealized life with Eddie. For the first two years of her life, he refused to be involved, but eventually he learned how to be a loving father. He was her hero; a warm, tender, affectionate Christian businessman who was married and living in a beautiful large home overlooking the waters of Puget Sound in Washington.

But when Mo was 11, her father, who'd recently been suffering from a constellation of devastating symptoms, was diagnosed with ALS and died soon after. Like any little girl losing her father, she was in shock. She cried a lot, didn't eat, and spent a lot of time alone.

Classic grieving process. I made sure she knew I was there when she needed me, but she tended to prefer being in her room. All I could do was give her time to work her way through her emotions.

I bought her a cell phone because she had to walk home from school and was alone every day for about half an hour before I got home from work. I also allowed her to use the computer in my room to play games.

One morning we were snuggled up side by side on my bed watching some silly cartoon when her phone rang. Assuming it was a girlfriend, I picked it up to hand it to her–then I saw the out-of-state area code. She grabbed it out of my hand and jumped out of bed.

"Who's calling from out of state?" I asked.

"Nobody, Mom." She turned her back and mumbled incoherently into the phone. She ended the call quickly, and when she turned back to me, her face was flushed and she wouldn't meet my eyes.

"What's going on? Who was that?" I demanded. Before she could answer, I snatched the phone out of her hand.

"Mom!" Frantic, she tried to take it back, even clawed at my arm as I held it overhead. "It's a boy, Mom! He's a friend and he likes me. Please Mom, please don't call him."

I was already dialing. She started to cry. The voice that answered belonged to not a boy but a man. "This is Moriyah's mom," I said, keeping my voice steady and calm, hoping to get as much information out of him as possible.

"Oh um… ya," he stammered.

"My daughter says you've been talking to her," I said. "How old are you, and what's your name?"

"My name… my name's Reggie. And I'm… I'm seventeen."

"If you're seventeen, then I'm Miss. America," I snapped. "What do you want with her?"

"We just talk. We're just friends, that's all."

"My daughter doesn't need any friends who are men! She's only eleven years old!"

"Eleven? She told me she was sixteen!" He sounded indignant that he'd been lied to. "How was I supposed to know that she—"

"I've got your phone number, and I'm calling the police right now!" I hung up.

Moriyah threw herself across the bed, sobbing. "Thanks a lot, Mom! That was my boyfriend! He said he loves me!"

"Loves you?" I was shaking with fear and rage. "He doesn't even know you! Unless… Mo, you haven't met him anywhere, have you?" She shook her head.

"Tell me the truth!" I sat her on the bed and glared. "How did this happen?"

"I met him on the computer," she admitted, sniffling back tears. "He's nice, Mom. Okay, so he's in high school. He's not that much older…"

"He's probably older than I am! Moriyah, he's one of those gross men who meet young girls on line and then…" a horrible thought hit me. "You didn't tell him where you live, did you?"

When she looked away, I knew she had. It turned out she had also told him what school she went to. He had told her he loved her and was going to visit her. Even though in that moment she didn't feel like being hugged, I grabbed her and held her tight anyway. The counselor in me knew she was having a reaction to her father's death, and looking for a replacement. The mother in me wanted to hunt him down and kill him.

I dialed 911 and reported the incident. But the officer replied, "Unless the guy specifically arranged a meeting with her, he's done nothing illegal."

"Well then I'm going to call that bastard and—"

"I wouldn't advise you do that, Ma'am. Since he hasn't crossed the line, he could accuse you of harassing him."

"So what he did is just okay?"

"It's not okay, it's just not illegal. Guys like this know the law. As long as they just talk and don't act, we can't go after them."

"But…"

"If your daughter is only eleven, maybe she shouldn't have her own phone. I got a daughter whose twelve and I'd never let her have a phone. Also, you shouldn't let your daughter spend so much time on the computer. Have to be careful these days. Watch everything they do."

I told him the reason she had a phone, and I told him the computer was in my bedroom and every time I checked, she was playing games on it.

"This is what I hear all the time from parents," he said. "Tell you what. My partner and I can come out and talk to her. Put a little scare in her. Would you like that?"

"That would be great," I said. "She needs a dose of reality."

They arrived within the hour. Moriyah, sitting sullen on the couch with her arms folded, didn't even look up.

"Ma'am, would it be okay if we talk to her alone for a few?"

Disappointed, I nodded, and went down the hall to busy myself in the kitchen. About twenty minutes later he and his partner appeared in the doorway.

"She's a great kid," he said. "Smart. But sometimes even the smart ones don't do the right thing. She said her dad died recently. Obviously she's looking for a new father figure. Is there a male in the family that could spend a little time with her?"

"I'll ask my mother's husband," I said.

"Good. She'll be okay. Call us if you need anything."

"Okay. Thank you so much." I walked them to the door, then called my mother and told her what happened. Then I called my sister and her husband and told them. And one by one, they all sat down with Moriyah and talked about the danger she'd put herself in, and that if she needed to talk, she should talk to family, not strangers. Everyone was calm and loving, and Moriyah listened and agreed.

But even though she never repeated the behavior, she continued to be angry and defiant. When it came time to start junior high, she simply refused to go. She had always been a straight A student, but now she said there was no reason for her to go to school. She locked her bedroom door and wouldn't let me in. Eventually I was able to get her to go back, but she was nasty and hostile. I called a meeting with her teacher to discuss her missed schoolwork, and her teacher was surprised to hear what was happening at home. She said Mo acted like everything was fine.

I was crushed that she was leading two lives–this normal one at school, and the one at home that kept me shut out. "Please talk to me," I kept saying. "I love you, and I want to help you!" But the more I begged, the more it infuriated her. Every ounce of rage she felt about the sudden death of her father was directed at me.

Yes, on a logical level, I understood this. But as a mother, I couldn't stop trying, to the point where we'd be screaming at each other; her furious, me in hysterics. Our biggest fights were about my demands that she see a counselor. Finally I got her to go; but her first therapist terminated their sessions after four unsuccessful attempts, reporting that she was non-cooperative, sat in silence, or responded in monosyllables. Upon the recommendation of the first therapist, I took her to a second therapist who specialized in childhood grief. The second therapist told me she also believed Moriyah had an Adjustment Disorder due to her father's death, but Mo didn't like her either, and refused to speak to her. In a last-ditch effort for intervention, I made her go with me to a grief support group. She met with other grieving kids, and I met with the grieving parents.

When the meeting was over I asked if she'd like to go again. "It's better than sitting in a room with a counselor," she said. A break through? I felt a trickle of hope, which I hid from her. *We'll see how it goes next week*, I thought.

Then a few days later, the building burned down (arson) and the program was put on hold. "What about holding it somewhere else?" I asked the director. "Or can you give me a referral to another place that's having these meetings?" He told me to wait a few months and check back.

So I waited. The months became years, and there wasn't much improvement in her attitude. Each time I brought up giving counseling another try she glared at me with daggers in her eyes and told me there was nothing wrong with her, that she was just a teenager and I was overreacting. "Your worrying drives me crazy," she'd say. "I'm getting good grades, I have friends, I don't do drugs, I'm home every night, I'm not out having sex with anyone. What do you want from me?"

I couldn't argue with any of that. All I could do was hope she'd outgrow her teenage "sulk."

Two summers after her father died, Moriyah was invited to spend a few weeks with a girlfriend she knew from visits with her dad in Washington. She had a group of friends there, and was excited about getting to see them again. I was excited too. Maybe a couple of weeks away would pull her out of her depression.

I called every few days to check in with her, and ask if she was having fun. "Yeah," she'd say, but nothing more. "Sleeping okay? Eating okay?" I probed. "Yeah, fine," she'd say. "I have to go."

I was worried sick. "Something is wrong," I told Rachael. "I hear it in her voice."

Sure enough, after about a week, she called to say that the girl she was staying with had been mean, and she wanted to come home. "What happened?" I asked. "Nothing," she said, "I just want to leave." We made the necessary arrangements, and then I called the girl's mother to find out what was going on. She had no idea.

When Moriyah got home, she kissed me and hugged me, but seemed distracted. I did her laundry, and when I took the basket into her room, I froze in the doorway. She pulled a blanket over her legs, but it was too late–I had already seen the burns.

"You're supposed to knock! This is my room!" she yelled.

I set the laundry basket down and sat on the edge of her bed. Tears welled up in my eyes, but I stayed calm. "Moriyah... what happened that you felt you had to do this to yourself?"

She lowered her head, shamed. "We had a fight. She made me feel shitty about myself. I burned my legs with the iron when she left the house."

I held her and stroked her back. My heart felt like it was collapsing.

I promptly scheduled an appointment for her with a counselor, but a few days before the appointment I received a call saying her medical insurance would not cover her counseling treatment after all, due to cutbacks in benefits. Moriyah promised that she would never, ever hurt herself again. I didn't have the money to pay out-of-pocket for counseling, so we agreed that if she ever hurt herself again there would be no second chance; I would take her straight to a psychiatric hospital. She nodded and swore it would never happen again. She said she had never hurt herself before, and only did it because the girl who had once been a best friend had rejected and excluded her. I wanted so much to believe that she would get better that I said, "*Promise*," and she said, "I promise." And for a little while she seemed better; she seemed to be trying to make an effort.

But when she was a sophomore in high school, her depression got worse. She was immobilized to the point that she couldn't get out of bed to go to school anymore. I gave her a choice: either return to counseling, or I'd take her to see a doctor. Though she was fuming at me for making her see a professional, she chose to

43

see a doctor, and began taking anti-depressants. I noted that the doctor had written, "Clinical Depression" and "Adjustment Disorder" as the diagnosis on her paperwork.

My father's grandmother, my father's mother (Grandma Bea), my father's father, and my mother's mother and father (holding hands).

My father Ronald Spencer
In 1969.

My parents on their wedding day
in 1963.

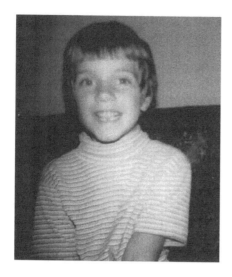

At age 5 or 6, I was confused by my Grandma Bea's erratic behavior. Visiting her in the sanatorium was very traumatic for me.

My Uncle Dan and my mother with their parents, my Grandma Ruth and my Grandpa Leon.

My mother's parents were a happy couple who rescued us when Dad's drinking got bad.

We could have been
any normal Christian family,
except that Dad mostly
stayed home with us kids
while Mom ran her own hair
salon and supported us.
Dad was a sheet metal
worker, but always wound
up quitting or getting fired.
I'm in the middle between
my sister Rhonda
and my brother David.

A graduate of
El Molino High School
In Forestville, CA
1983.

47

In 1996 I became pregnant with Mo despite the fact that I was a lesbian, had no intention of marrying her father, only had sex with him twice, and used contraception both times. I always felt I was meant to have her.

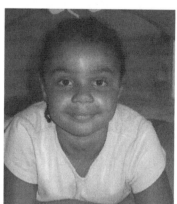

For years I unfairly depended on Mo to keep me sane. Even during my deepest depression she gave me a reason to keep going.

With her father in 2007 at the Daddy-Daughter Dance.
She adored him and worshiped him the way little girls do.
Compared to me, he lived a calm, stable life.

Mo's struggles with her weight and her mixed ethnicity contributed to her depression.

I always thought that this selfie of Mo at aged 15 really captured the sadness in her eyes.

Mo hated having her picture taken, and I'm so glad to have this photo of the two of us together on Easter 2013, just a few months before she died.

My beautiful daughter.

This is the Memorial Tree,
a heavy crystal vase
filled with water and glass stones,
that mysteriously tipped over
in the middle of the night.

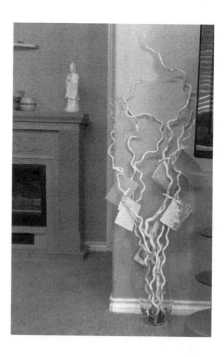

CHAPTER FOUR

THE ALARM WENT OFF and as I stumbled into the kitchen, desperate for my morning coffee, I heard Romeo yapping and jumping against Mo's bedroom door. I opened it and he dashed out, but to my surprise, Mo wasn't in bed. Panic and dread swept through me. I looked in her bathroom, but it was empty. I saw that the back sliding glass door was open, and all I could think was that someone had broken in and kidnapped her. Terrified, I turned to go wake Rachael.

And that's when I noticed my daughter's knee jutting out from inside of her closet. Feeling sick, I stepped over to the closet, and saw her body hanging lifeless; dangling inches above the floor. She was stiff, blue and cold, her face twisted, grotesque and lifeless. I heard screaming from somewhere outside of my body. "No! Moriyah, no!"

Running into my bedroom, I shook Rachael to wake her. Rachael sprang to her feet and followed me into Mo's room. I kept screaming her name, over and over, staring into her blank, glassy eyes.

I don't remember how long it was before the police and ambulance arrived; I have foggy memories of being helped up off the floor by what I was told later were "bereavement workers"– softspoken older ladies whose sad eyes said they knew my inconsolable pain. They guided me to the dining room table. One of them held my hand as if I were a lost child. Part of me was embarrassed by it, but another part of me needed the reassuring touch of another human being, even if a stranger. I thought, *I need my mother. Where is my mother?*

The coroner, a man who looked like detective Hercule Poirot in his snappy straw hat and matching linen suit, confirmed that she had died the night before, not long after we had gone to bed. "She didn't suffer long," he assured me. I wondered if that was true or if he was just being kind. He handed me a suicide note that said she had dreamed of Heaven and her father, and that she was "done with this life." The EMTs wheeled her out in a body bag, and when the police and the coroner and the bereavement team left, I felt myself slide off the seat, onto the floor; wailing.

I called her doctor and demanded answers. He said gently, "Moriyah told me she wasn't having suicidal thoughts, so it could be that this particular anti-depressant backfired and increased her suicidal thoughts, which happens sometimes. But you just never know with teenagers. I wish there was something I could say. I'm just so sorry." I hung up, furious and disgusted, but deep down gratified to share the blame. He was her *doctor*! He should have seen this coming!

In the days that followed, I tried to come to grips with what had happened. My mind kept repeating, *This can't be real... this is a nightmare... I'll wake up and I'll go into her room and wake her and hold her and tell her I love her... and she'll be annoyed and say, "Mom, I'm fine!"* For a week I wandered from room to room; in a daze, heart dead. The one room I didn't go in was hers. I couldn't even look at the closed door. I resumed smoking. I answered the phone and read sympathy cards, and nodded when everyone assured me that it had not been my fault, that I had been a good mother.

A good mother. Living with the guilt of her death was torture. I couldn't talk to anyone, not even Rachael; in my journal I wrote, *An atom bomb has been dropped, and I am melting in the blast.* I felt completely dissociated from the world. The only emotion I was in touch with was a pain so deep that sometimes I couldn't even catch my breath. One morning I got up, went into the bathroom, and vomited. Then I lay on the bathroom floor while the room spun sickeningly.

As the days turned to weeks, my mind was in a state of escalating madness. I wrote poetry and indulged in crying jags. I paced like a caged animal, back and forth, back and forth while I went over every single detail like a forensic investigator, trying to piece together the dark mystery. I walked the hallway past her bathroom, hoping like a crazy person that I'd bump into her the way we used to. Once I made myself look in, and was startled to see her lips prints on the bottom of her mirror; beautiful full lips that had kissed the mirror in a moment of frivolous teen girlisheness. It was almost as if she was kissing me goodbye. I pressed my face to the mirror, sobbing, "Come back! I miss you! I need you! Please come back!"

I developed a phobia about falling asleep. I felt I had to stay awake as long as humanly possible. The first month I barely even shut my eyes. *Don't fall asleep,* my brain said. *Look what happened the last time you fell asleep! Your daughter killed herself!*

Logically I knew that at some point I was going to have to stop obsessing about her. But I couldn't shake the feeling that if I stopped obsessing, it would diminish my love for her. And I felt so responsible; to stop obsessing would mean that I forgave myself, and I was nowhere near ready to do that.

I found myself wishing I could die, too. Not that I wanted to take my own life; but just that… maybe if I was out driving and a car plowed into mine and killed me. Or if I got a terrible disease and died. Then I could be with her. And I wouldn't have to live with the grief and the guilt. In my chaotic, crazy state of mind, it made sense.

Then, a month later, as I sat staring at the pretty purple urn I'd picked out for Moriyah's ashes, I realized that somehow I would have to find a way to make peace with the nightmare that had become my life.

"Let's go to the local Farmer's Market," Rachael suggested. "Have lunch and enjoy the sun. Summer is almost over." "Okay," I said, but I didn't get up.

"Do you realize you haven't left the house in two months?" I shrugged. It was true.

"Come on." She nudged my foot with hers. "Let's go."

Reluctantly I stood, put on my shoes, and followed her out. Right away I was glad; the fresh air smelled sweeter than ever. Immediately I felt guilty about feeling good, but Rachael took my hand and squeezed it. "Okay?" she asked. "Okay," I said.

We strolled along, stopping at endless stands to select ears of corn, nectarines and apples, and browsing the homemade craft items.

I heard giggles, and looking up, I saw a group of young women in their early twenties, and in the middle was Moriyah, carefree and laughing at some story she was telling, speaking in her voice, the happy center of attention. I felt myself sway; my knees buckled, and if I hadn't reached out to grab Rachael, I would have fallen. I felt Rachael's body jerk, and heard her say, "That girl looks just like Moriyah!"

We stood, frozen, as this vision headed right for us; then she floated past, as if she couldn't see us, as if we were the ones who weren't real. Rachael opened her mouth, and I knew she was going to say Moriyah's name, but before she could, as much as I wanted to stay, I pulled on her arm. "Come on, let's go."

"But..."

"Come on." I don't know why I didn't go after the girl, I don't know why I didn't reach out and touch her shoulder and say, "Please wait, please tell me..." Tell me what? *It wasn't her, it was just*

56

a girl who looked like her. But I knew it was her, it was somehow her...
thriving on the Other Side; now a little older. And happy–so happy.

For several seconds, I couldn't move. Rachael turned around as
if to call her, but before she could, I grabbed her by the arm and got
us walking in the opposite direction. We were both so stunned that
months would pass before we would speak of it.

I contacted a support group for parents whose teen had
committed suicide, but after speaking with the well-meaning–but
under-qualified–facilitator who had no formal education in
counseling or psychology, I wondered about the wisdom of
revealing I was a counselor. I feared that my integrity would be
questioned because of the unspoken expectations people have of
counselors: (1) We should be nice all the time (2) We should always
stop to listen and be interested when people share their troubles (3)
We should always be positive and understanding (4) We are allowed
to have problems, but not big, huge, horrible problems. And (5)
Above all, we must stay calm at all times and function well in a
crisis.

As soon as I decided not to share the information that I was a
counselor, I made the decision not to join a group.

I also made the decision to feel like a huge fake and a huge
failure. A mental health coach whose beautiful, smart and promising
15 year old daughter had committed suicide... who could respect
someone like that? Like creeping vines, self-loathing wound its way
in a grip around my heart.

I also replayed the horror of finding her. Over and over and
over. Rachael admitted that she was having nightmares and vivid
flashbacks. I diagnosed us both with Post-Traumatic Stress, but
didn't know how to fix it. I wondered if I would always feel this
way.

In his classic *A Grief Observed,* Christian theologian C.S. Lewis
says, "Nobody ever told me grief felt so much like fear." Nailed it.
The fear I felt was immense and ever-present. It was like a hungry

lion that threatened to shred and devour what little remained of my self-esteem. There is so much shame attached to suicide, because of the guilt. *I could have done things differently. She would still be alive if only I had...*

Tragic endings have a widespread ripple effect. Not only was our family deeply impacted, but Moriyah's boyfriend and school friends expressed the trouble they were having processing their grief. One friend said, "I thought I knew her. It makes me doubt that I can trust anybody." I thought I knew her, too. Though she was struggling with depression, I'd always considered her an extremely level-headed and pragmatic person. She was a planner, and had a bright future mapped out. She was going to become a radiology technician, she was earning good grades, and spending two to three hours every night sequestered away with her algebra and chemistry. She'd just been nominated by a teacher at school to participate in a national medical forum, and would be spending two weeks at a California university medical school learning the latest cutting-edge medical technologies, and attending lectures of famous motivational speakers. She had plans to visit her older brother and sister while she was there. Her grandparents had paid her tuition, and she had an exciting life ahead of her.

But of course depression doesn't care about trips or visits or plans.

When I was cleaning out her room, I found a copy of *The Bell Jar* by Sylvia Plath. I'd had to read it in high school, and as I sat there, I flipped through it and reviewed the plot: a young girl named Esther is an academic success, but after losing her father, she becomes depressed. She tries several times to commit suicide, until her mother puts her into a mental hospital. Plath, via the voice of Esther, sums it up this way: "To the person in the bell jar, blank and stopped as a dead baby, the world itself is a bad dream."

Other items I found in her room completed the missing pieces of the puzzle. In her diary were written these prophetic words: *Nothing is ever what it seems.* Below that caption she had drawn a picture of a noose, complete with little flies buzzing around it, and a flyswatter. I anguished for her. How does one get to a place of caring so little about their own death that they can satirize it? On the next page she had drawn the devil saying, *Stop taking the pills.* Rachael counted her antidepressant and calculated that she had stopped taking them five days before her death. "And look at this," Rachael said, showing me a box that had been under the bed: I saw food diaries, a scale, and diuretics, including laxatives. (Later, some of her friends confirmed that she had been obsessing about her weight, and that she used to vomit every day after lunch).

"How could this have been going on?" I asked Rachael. "I remember when she started losing weight—I told her she was thin enough and to stop dieting. I even asked if she had an eating disorder, I asked her flat out and she said no!"

"You know yourself how sneaky someone can be when they're trying to conceal something," Rachael said. "I have to tell you something."

"What?"

"A few days after Mo died, I had a dream that she was being pulled between life and the afterlife. I saw her father in a white robe, glowing with health and strength, and he was asking Moriyah to come with him, and I was saying, *No, Moriyah, stay here!* She was having trouble making up her mind, I could tell… and then she said that even though she loved her earthly family and didn't want to hurt them, she wanted to go."

"So her dead father just comes and takes her?" I demanded, angry at him; then was startled at how crazy I sounded. Rachael put her hand on my shoulder. I buried my face in my hands and cried.

Because of my Christian upbringing and because I'd studied world religions, I knew that suicide was considered a sin which could damn a soul to eternal punishment. I couldn't bear the thought of my daughter suffering in the afterlife any more than she'd already suffered with mental illness. I hadn't attended a formal religious service since I had been excommunicated from the church for coming out as a lesbian, so I didn't have a pastor or a priest to talk to. One night, in a fit of what felt like madness, I went online and found a Ouija Board that was supposed to be able to make contact with the deceased. The few clear answers I got didn't seem to be anything Moriyah would say. But I had to do something. I had to speak to her one last time.

CHAPTER FIVE

A LOCAL SPIRITUAL MEDIUM that we had consulted in the past reached out to me through a networking site. Her name was Suzi, and after expressing her condolences, she said if there was anything she could do, to let her know. I enthusiastically responded and scheduled a session at my home. She'd been amazingly accurate with information in the past, and had been a source of spiritual strength and encouragement for both Moriyah and I. Nervous and excited, I couldn't wait for the day of the reading to arrive. When Suzi swept into the house (and that is the only way to describe her buoyant, confident energy), she said, "I've already had a visit from Moriyah."

"What? Tell me!"

"She's been hanging out with me all day, and there are two men who wish to speak to Rachael."

Rachael's eyes went wide; she'd lost two male relatives who were very dear to her.

"These two are very persistent, and they've pushed themselves to the front of the line," Suzi said. As she reported what she was being told, I waited impatiently. I felt like pulling my hair out! This was supposed to be about Moriyah!

Then suddenly Suzi stopped talking, listened a moment with her head cocked, and said, "Okay, Moriyah is here."

With that, I felt my body relax and take a sigh. There was a sudden quietness in the room, and a peace I hadn't felt in a long time. "She's showing me a round... like a clear globe," Suzi began. "It's like a crystal ball. She said it was special to her, and she wants me to have it."

Rachael and I exchanged glances. Crystal ball? Moriyah didn't have a crystal ball. "This morning we cleared out her room," I said. "We didn't see anything that was—"

But then Rachael said, "I know what she means—that snow globe!"

Our eyes went to the bag in the foyer that we'd filled with stuff to donate. Rachael ran over and pulled it out and held it up: It had a white horse inside, and a music box that played "As Time Goes By."

"This was a gift from her father," Suzi said (which was true.) "She wants me to have it for my altar."

"Altar?" asked Rachael not sure if she had read Suzi's lips correctly.

"I have an altar at home that has items from clients." Suzi wound the key and the song played, and it was a cheerful sound.

"Okay," I said.

"Something is bothering her," Suzi went on. She shut her eyes, as if listening very hard. "She says her body is in two different places. She wants her body together, not separated. Where are her ashes?"

That's when it really really hit me that Mo's spirit was in the room communicating with us. "I got two urns for her ashes," I said. "Her boyfriend wanted some..."

Suzi was shaking her head. "She wants the ashes all together in one urn."

"Okay," I said again. It was so unreal, it was just insanely unreal, to know that my daughter was right there in the room!

"This is important," Suzi said, "she wants to apologize for the way she left, and for the mess she left behind. She wants you to know that you did everything you could for her. You tried your best, and that's what counts. It wasn't your fault. She really wants you to know that."

I became aware of tears coming down my cheeks. This was almost word for word what her suicide note had said.

"You can't comprehend this now, but everything happened according to Moriyah's life plan, the way it was supposed to."

This was huge. If this was true, then it hadn't been my fault, it had been about decisions made maybe before my daughter had come into this incarnation. Mouth hanging open, I nodded.

"Once I was in communication with a girl who should not have been in this world. She always felt different, because she was. She never fit in because she wasn't from here." Suzi looked at Rachael. "Your soul is from a different galaxy. You're different, too. You're a lot like Mo."

I looked at Rachael, and she smiled knowingly. Yes, my fiancée was quite different, I was well aware of that. She'd expressed feelings of always being the outsider since childhood, deaf in a hearing world since the age of two. "Nina, the two souls closest to you don't belong to this particular Universe. But you do."

"But if Moriyah and I were so different, how come we were put together in this life?"

"In order to give both your souls an opportunity to achieve a kind of... it's hard to explain; it was for your souls' perfecting. Moriyah wasn't an emotional being, and she had trouble relating to you, because you are all about emotions. You feel emotions strongly and even chose a career that requires you to understand and dabble in the emotions of others."

This was true; I sometimes considered myself too emotional.

"Moriyah was from a galaxy in which emotions were no longer necessary," Suzi went on. "Her soul had evolved to the point where emotions were considered to be lower in value and just, well... immature. She agreed to come to Earth to learn patience and forbearance with lower-level beings."

I felt myself smile. Once I had asked Moriyah why she wanted to go into the medical field and work with technology not patients, and she said, "People irritate me. Machines don't. I want as little contact with people as possible." My sister had even given her a wallet that said, "I Hate People" with a grumpy-faced little character on it.

"Moriyah's father was her savior figure here on earth, but you and she were soul mates of a different kind."

I was so glad to hear this, having started to feel like a less evolved soul! "What kind of soul mates were we?"

"Soul mate relationships have a few defining characteristics," Suzi explained. "First, they always bring lessons with them. Some lessons are painful, while others are positive. Your relationship was passionate. Intensely loving, stormy, painful and profound—a deep exchange, not a surface one."

"Exchange?"

"A soul exchange is a relationship in which you learn a lesson via another soul's involvement in your life. Soul mates often bring difficult lessons, and they'll always uncover your true nature to you." "That sounds right," Rachael said.

"Secondly, a tell-tale sign of a soul mate is that the relationship is marked by turbulence, and is often transient, meaning the nature of the relationship is so intense that it may not be long lasting. Like a fire ablaze, these are intense relationships which burn out quickly—and sometimes leave you feeling burned. Buddhists believe these soul exchanges are given to us to work out our karma with the help of the soul mate."

"So I was just as much of a soul mate to her as her father was?"

"Absolutely! Your relationship was like rough waters. With him, it was calm seas."

"So she ended her life because she accomplished what she came here to?" I asked.

Suzi shook her head. "Unfortunately, no. She's going to have to come back."

I sat back and tried to digest it all.

Suzi shifted in her seat and said, "Our session is complete. Let's go celebrate Moriyah."

So we went to Mo's favorite pizza place and ordered a pitcher of her favorite soda. I even set a place for her at the table to honor the place she'd held in our lives. The grief wasn't over, but it was a relief to have some answers.

CHAPTER SIX

THEY CALL THEM GRIEF ATTACKS, those moments when
sorrow engulfs you. Maybe a specific memory triggers it, or maybe
it just hits you out of nowhere, like a tornado the meteorologists
didn't see coming. One slammed into me on what would have been
Mo's 16th birthday, two months after her suicide. My parents had
been planning a big sweet 16 birthday party for her at their new
home, and as the day approached, my mother and I were so
devastated that we only emailed one another; it was too painful to
even talk about it. Like the aftershock that follows an earthquake, it
hit me full force and left me emotionally reeling for days. I had
several intense flashbacks and didn't sleep.

The morning of her birthday I scribbled out these lines in the
sweet sixteen card I bought:

Sweet Sixteen:
It's your birthday
We had planned to celebrate but you couldn't wait to grow up
Now I can't sleep at night, because I did that night
and you never woke up.
Part of me still believes if I hadn't gone to sleep it wouldn't have happened.
Part of me is still living in terror.
This house is like a jail cell; everywhere I turn I smell you, see you.

I still wear makeup that you once wore because I read somewhere that
our cells are still in it mingling with my cells
Somehow that is the smallest of comforts
that we can still touch if only in the minutest of ways.
How do I celebrate the ashes left behind?
I thought I'd survived the tidal wave
Now I see there's other, smaller waves that are rolling in.
Thank God I'm a strong swimmer
because sometimes in moments like these
when the guilt is piled up so high that it eclipses the sun,
I want to glimpse you again and be reminded of your
beauty and sharp wit and the way you would quietly whisper
"mama" when you needed me.
Happy Birthday, baby.

After that, I pushed myself to return to work. As my first new client recounted her profound anxiety and depression after her husband's death four years ago, tears of empathy and understanding filled my eyes. Over the years I'd learned to control my emotions during counseling regardless of my personal feelings, but I felt her pain keenly. The other thing I was aware of was my own relative stability; I felt validated that compared to her, I was healing more effectively.

When she lowered her head and said, "I don't know if you can understand how horrible I feel," I reached out for her hand, and shared my story. Her eyes grew wide as she listened, and I knew she was thinking *If she can get through her loss, I can get through mine.* We both cried.

But after she left, I realized that there was a good chance this would happen again, and that anytime a client talked about depression, an eating disorder, loss of a loved one, or suicidal thoughts, I would wind up reliving my own pain. Regretfully, I gave my notice, and then I let my other clients know that I could not continue to see them either. My heart felt like it was breaking; I felt once again like a failure—I had let Moriyah down, and now I was letting down my clients. And myself. For the past decade I had only been schooled and employed in one subject: mental health. I was steeped in debt, without a game plan. And while I didn't expect a fairytale ending after Mo's suicide, I had assumed that once I turned the corner, I would be able to resume my life and career.

I started doing the *How much can one person take?* thing. A lot. I went back to blaming myself. As a professional, I knew that my daughter's suicide had been a perfect storm of mental illness, existential teen angst, and immaturity. I wish I had said, "You're only 15. You haven't lived long enough to see that time always brings an answer." I wish so much I had said that.

As a counselor, I had read about grief. I was familiar with the five steps—Denial, Anger, Bargaining, Depression and Acceptance—and while it's true that we go through those emotions, I didn't realize until Mo's death that it's so much more complicated. The steps make it sound as if once you get to the end of one, you have conquered it and just go into the next one. But I felt myself go through them all and back again to the first one. Over and over and over. Many times I thought I achieved the peace that comes with Acceptance, only to find myself absolutely blind with fury at God just a few hours later.

Unemployed and still struggling, I learned why trauma survivors often develop agoraphobia; there are too many things in the real world that can trigger a memory, and therefore, pain. For months I hid at home with Rachael and Romeo, Mo's puppy. The three of us nursed each other's wounds as best we knew how. Already a homebody, Rachael didn't mind staying home, but watching me suffer was hard for her. My moods alternated from crushing depression, anger, guilt and shame, and then the anxiety, which I thought I had I left behind that day at the airport, came flooding back.

I realized that I would not be "pushing through the pain," or speeding through this process. Nor would I be taking any unnecessary risks for a while. I realized that my comeback would be slow and steady. If I could make a comeback at all.

CHAPTER SEVEN

LIKE THE OLD SAYING GOES, "Denial's not just a river in Egypt;" indeed, denial is *everywhere*. Victims of domestic violence stay with their partner. Addicts insist they need alcohol or drugs in order to get through the day. Diabetics continue to eat sugar, obese people keep stopping at McDonalds on their way home, insecure people keep having plastic surgery in an effort to stop the aging process. But when we pretend we don't have a problem, what we're denying can manifest as depression. Express or suppress.

Because of Mo's sudden and violent death, I didn't have time to prepare myself psychologically. It was as if in the moment I found her body, my eyes refused to believe what they were seeing. My brain could not process all the horror. This anesthetic-like reaction is the brain's way of softening the blow. That's why when we recall a traumatic incident, it feels like time slowed down; the brain feeds the horrific circumstances to us at a slower rate. Similarly, denial is the conscious mind's way of slowing the absorption of pain. The problem is not in the denial, for it is, as Sigmund Freud explained, a defense mechanism which keeps pain at bay. It's like the scene in *When Harry Met Sally* where Sally tells her girlfriends that she and her fiancée broke up. She explains calmly that they wanted different things—she wanted to get married, and he didn't. They're impressed with how well she's taking it. A few years later she discovers he's engaged, and it hits her: He said he didn't want to get married, but what he meant was, he didn't want to marry *her*. Finally she breaks down and experiences the loss.

Bottom line–pain is poison. You have to get it out of your system somehow. Talk it out, exercise it out, journal it out, cry it out, yell it out, but whatever you do, don't deny it's there.

After Mo's suicide, anger was my go-to emotion for a long time. Sometimes I was mad at God for allowing this to happen. Usually I was mad at myself for having been so blind to her needs. There were even times I was mad at Mo for not asking for help. Finally, exhausted, drained, and not through the grief, I came to the conclusion that no amount of anger was going to change what had happened. I let go of feeling like the victim. I let go of feeling like a martyr. I let go of blaming God, myself, and my daughter.

When everything's taken from you, everything you really cared about or loved, when there isn't any more that life could do to break you, my advice is to just surrender. Like getting caught in a riptide, our first instinct is to swim against it. But we can't outswim a riptide; we can only stop struggling and allow it to take us. Eventually, we'll reach calmer waters.

And that's how I chose to be something that wasn't fashionable or flashy or powerful or potent. In the deepest part of me, for once, I just wanted to be... real.

Just months after Moriyah's death I began to see how I might be able to use this suffering to my advantage; transform the pain so that it could create positive change in my life. The first step was a willingness to "sit with my pain." The longer I sat quietly and allowed myself to fully feel it (pass the tissues, please), the more I began to see pain as my most esteemed teacher and my greatest friend. My consciousness was opened to see how all things suffer, and how my pain was no better or worse, bigger or smaller than anyone else's pain. I understood that there is only the shared pain of living, and we are all brothers and sisters, toiling shoulder to shoulder in this tattered cotton field. Today I can testify to the transformative power of pain. The horrifying, excruciating feelings I didn't think I could survive have ultimately produced growth.

So my next big step toward healing was being grateful for the pain. There is growing interest and research in a phenomenon called "post-traumatic growth," that is, positive change resulting from trauma. People experiencing post-traumatic growth report that they have stronger personal relationships, an increased appreciation of life, greater inner strength, deeper spirituality and more sense of being connected to a Big Picture. A cancer survivor, for example, might truly recognize how precious and beautiful life is. A rape victim might discover that she is stronger emotionally than she thought, and can build upon that new sense of empowerment. Post-traumatic growth is the natural direction of successful working-through.

The opposite of post-traumatic growth is "negative ruminating;" brooding about guilt, shame, or anger. Negative ruminating is characterized by replaying the "I should have…" loop over and over, without resolution.

There are some things we can do to be proactive in developing positive responses to grief. Researchers have found that optimism, social support, spirituality and positive coping skills enable post-traumatic growth. Relaxation and breathing exercises when we're anxious, and gratitude exercises (pondering all we've learned in spite of the pain) were also shown to increase post-traumatic growth. I mentioned earlier that I had to be willing to "sit with my pain." I meant that I did a fair amount of what is known as "reflective pondering" to help me assign meaning to my experience.

It's this post-traumatic growth that leads to gratitude.

I'm not saying the process is easy. We humans tend to cling to the three great energy robbers–anger, resentment and regret–because they're familiar, comfortable. It's why we keep telling stories of past trauma and victimizations to others; it helps us justify our fears, insecurities, phobias and hang ups that lead to our lack of engagement in life. And don't forget about the two Big Payoffs—attentions and sympathy.

One of my mentors explained it this way, "Most of us would rather 'be right' than go for an expanded result." In other words, I can "be right" and insist that I'm never going to recover from my losses or trauma, or I can choose to let go of the victim mentality, and embrace healing. While I experienced feelings of anger towards my daughter for her suicide (a normal response, and a part of the grief healing cycle), I realized it was not going to benefit me to take on the role of a victim, and use her death as an excuse to become a passive observer of life.

Why is it that some people seem to be super-resilient, bouncing back no matter how much life throws at them, able to find beauty amidst the ashes, while other people harden and become cynical, angry, or feel victimized? In his best-selling book, *The Resiliency Advantage*, (2005), the late Al Siebert, PhD, believes that "highly resilient people are flexible, adapt to new circumstances quickly, and thrive in constant change. Most important, they expect to bounce back and feel confident that they will. They have a knack for creating good luck out of circumstances that many others see as bad luck." Psychologists assert that it's possible for all of us to learn to bounce back from adversity, even the soul-crushing kind. Barbara Fredrickson, PhD, the author of *Positivity* (2009) points out that when life circumstances turn sour, less-resilient people feel their whole world has gone wrong. This is what is known as, "catastrophizing," or thinking in all-or-nothing terms. If I was a catastrophic thinker, I'd claim that my daughter's suicide was a tragedy from which I'll never be able to recover. And while my life has undoubtedly been profoundly and negatively altered by her choice, the truth is that it is up to me whether I allow myself to be overwhelmed and overcome by the grief. I can focus on my loss, or I can focus on recovery.

Organismic theorist Kurt Goldstein coined the term "self-actualization" to refer to an organism's drive to "actualize itself as fully as possible," but Abraham Maslow personalized it (and got credit for it) when he proposed the Self-Actualized personality. Self-actualizing individuals show significantly lower levels of anxiety and depression following trauma, and experience an "internal locus of control." In other words, they see themselves as being responsible for their own happiness, and look within for direction, instead of depending upon others for direction. A person with an internal locus of control believes that forces shaping one's life are largely within one's control, and while they understand that they can't always control events, they can always make the choice about how to react. They see themselves as the architects of their own lives.

CHAPTER EIGHT

ON THE ONE-YEAR ANNIVERSARY of Mo's death I was sitting at my desk still revisiting the event–had I really done all I could, or could I have stopped it? I should have counted her pills like Rachael said; I should have made her go to therapy, I should have taken her straight to the hospital–when I heard *tap tap tap* on my window. I looked up and saw a small brown bird. I went back to my lamenting, and a few minutes later I heard it again: *tap tap tap*. Again, I looked up, and I saw a different bird–this one is brown with white and tan feathers. Weird.

That night something woke me from a sound sleep at 3:00 am. I felt the familiar warm fuzziness of my dog Romeo pressed against my leg. But all at once he woke with a jerk, leapt out of bed and dashed to the front door, growling and barking. Alarmed, I got up and followed him. The motion-activated porch light flooded the yard. I peeked out the blinds, but didn't see anything.

"What is it, Romeo?" I asked. He was freaked out and it took a while to make him stop barking.

In the morning I told the landlord about it. "Sometimes geese come up from the lake and set it off," he said.

"At 3:00 in the morning?"

"Coyotes, then," he said. "I've seen coyotes."

I asked him to review the security video tape. He told me later that the video didn't show anything that should have activated the light. "Must have just gone on for no reason," he said.

I woke at the same time the next night, and lay there wondering if the light was going to come on again, and then I heard a *crash!* in the living room. Romeo started barking and jumped off the bed; a ten pound squirt with an exaggerated sense of being big and scary who stands up to dogs three times his size, he began to whimper and got back in bed. "It's okay," I said, stroking him. For some reason I was convinced it was nothing to worry about, and fell right back to sleep. I dreamed of being taken to another place, a place so interesting that I happily followed. A smiling guide led me down a mountainside towards a village, down, down, down the stony path we headed, toward an exciting, intriguing adventure waiting for me below.

In the morning, I got up and searched the house for anything out of place or broken. Nothing. I joined Rachael in the kitchen and told her about the crash I heard.

She looked startled. "When I got up this morning, Moriyah's memorial tree was lying on its side."

We sat and stared at each other. The tree was in a glass vase filled with stones and weighed several pounds. How would something that heavy fall over in the middle of the night all by itself?

Later that afternoon we were in the living room, and the TV turned itself on. Startled, we looked at the TV, at the remote sitting on the coffee table, and then at each other. There was no sound, just picture. Without saying a word, I stood and went into my office. I sat at my desk and looked at my books, where things were logical and made sense. Scientifically-yielded data backed up by facts, research, and results that could be replicated in any lab. And then suddenly the TV was blaring. I ran back out to the living room. As a deaf person, Rachael wouldn't have bothered to turn up the volume–and sure enough, she was just sitting there, and the remote had not been moved from the coffee table.

"I'm going out for a walk," I announced, and left quickly. *This is Moriyah, her spirit is here; she's trying to communicate with us*, I thought; or have I just gone crazy? "Okay," I said out loud, "If this is you, turn the TV off now." I walked a little bit, then turned around and went back inside. When Rachael saw me she said, "The TV shut itself off while you were gone."

I dreaded going to bed that night. Romeo knew something was up, because for the first time ever, he slept under the bed. Rachael kissed me goodnight and dropped off quickly. After tossing and turning for a couple of hours, I finally fell asleep. But just before 3:00 am I woke to the sound of someone knocking. It didn't really sound like it was at the door; it sounded like knocking that filled the room. I lay there, frozen with fear, and then the kitchen light came on...shut off... on... off... six times. Terrified, I woke Rachael and told her.

"Just think happy thoughts," she advised sleepily. "Pretend you're in the tropics."

"The tropics?" I repeated, but she had shut her eyes. I lay awake the rest of the night, finally getting up early to begin researching.

The first book I read about was *Childlight: How Children Reach out to Their Parents from the Beyond* by Donna Theisen. Her son Michael had died suddenly in an auto accident, and she was so convinced that the "signs" she experienced were his spirit that she conducted 40 interviews with other parents who had gone through the same thing. I kept searching and found other accounts of after-death contacts. A CNN news story titled, "Do loved ones bid farewell from beyond the grave," told the story of a hairdresser who was visited by a friend, only to find out that he had died 9 hours earlier. She claimed that he'd come by to thank her for all the help she'd given him: "*I think he felt he had some unfinished business and couldn't leave without saying goodbye.*"

I learned that twenty percent of Americans, some 50 million people, feel they've been the recipient of an after-death contact, but most don't tell anyone because they're afraid others will think they've gone off the deep end. Many feel that spirits visited them for a specific reason, as with the hairdresser.

Do Moriyah and I have some unfinished business to settle? I wondered. As soon as I asked myself this, I knew the answer: My daughter didn't want me to feel guilty.

I was two mothers—one good, and one I've come to think of as "weak." But as I sat back and re-examined the blame I assigned myself, I saw that my motives were pure—never for one moment did I ever ignore Mo's suffering. I tried to get her help. What I had to own was my desperate love for her; a love so needy that I was scared I would lose her if I pushed her too hard. After my attempts to reach her were rejected, I stopped confronting her. I was too insecure to stand up to the seething anger she directed at me. And she had every right to be angry. Because of my rocky love life, every adult she got close to eventually left, so she struggled with letting others in. Also, she witnessed her father, the one person she could count on to stick around, die a horrible death. These losses left her unable or unwilling to become attached to others. Had she been able to trust that others would be there for her, she might have risked telling me or someone else what she was going through. We know we can be our worst selves with those who love us the most, because we trust they are not going to abandon us, and during her teens, Moriyah let me see her dark side. But after the losses piled up, she stopped trusting me. Me, the one who should have helped her with the rage, betrayal, loneliness, and depression. Me, the professional, successful emotional counselor. But the thought of admitting all the dark and hideous thoughts and feelings she was having must have filled her with dread and shame. She couldn't let me see how sick her mind had become because she didn't want to be reduced to the status of one of my patients. She didn't want to disappoint me, and felt she couldn't let down her family who had such high hopes and expectations of her. As her diary prophesied, nothing is ever what it seems. Her brain had turned on her and had begun to self-destruct. So she took the only way out that seemed remotely dignified to her, and that was to exit before any of us could discover the truth of how ill she really was. She took her life so the last of her self-respect could remain intact. What Moriyah did not know at age 15 was that all of us have felt ashamed, pathetically weak, and at times terrified by our own thoughts. Had she taken the wall down and allowed me to look in, I would have assured her of that. It wasn't the depression which took her life; ultimately, it was the shame.

In the final analysis, we let each other down. And while I came to understand and accept that I wasn't a horrible mother, I had to find a way to forgive myself for not figuring this all out when I had her.

On the third night after Mo's anniversary, I started thinking about Grace. Grace means "unmerited favor;" in other words, forgiveness. Was I deserving of grace? I went to bed late, and slept soundly.

In the morning, I checked my social media site and clicked on the app. that delivers a daily personalized "Message from God." And this was what I saw: *On this day, God wants you to know that it is time for you to finally forgive yourself. You've carried the guilt, the shame for long enough. You've kept your wounds open for long enough. The time has come to let go, to heal. Keep the lessons and let the pain heal. Yes, you know what I'm talking about.*

I shut my eyes and whispered a prayer that my mother taught me; a prayer when you want to forgive, but can't muster the courage: *Make me willing to be willing to forgive myself, totally and completely.*

Moriyah came back because she wanted me to know that letting her go wasn't the same as forgetting her. But even as I write this, I know that grief is a journey, and that setbacks will occur.

Some days I feel satisfied with myself, and others days I slip back to feeling self-loathing and angry with myself. I've got to expect these feelings will arise from time to time, so the best approach is to be gentle with my progress. I had received a message from God, alright, but more importantly, Moriyah had hand delivered it.

CHAPTER NINE

RATHER THAN "KEEP BUSY," the advice I heard most after Mo's death, I recommend the opposite–make time to grieve. Don't try to rush yourself through it. Just as the body needs time to heal after a major injury, so do the mind and emotions. I will grieve on and off for the rest of my life, but I don't have to set up camp there. Allowing myself to fully feel my grief when it drops in for visit is a way of honoring my daughter's life and our connection, while giving into hopelessness is not. Giving myself permission to grieve is self-care, just as giving myself permission to rest when I'm on overwhelm or fatigued is self-care. Giving myself permission to go out and enjoy nature and fun recreational activities is self-care. Giving myself permission to be close and sexually intimate again is self-care. Giving myself permission to cook healthy meals and exercise is self-care. Giving myself permission to clean and organize the house is self-care. Giving myself leisure time to read a book, soak in the tub, listen to music, or watch a movie is self-care. In all these ways I am sending a message to myself, "It's okay to take care of yourself and enjoy living again."

When we grieve, especially if we have been harboring guilt, we are tempted to stop experiencing life in its fullness. This is known as "survivor's guilt." A part of us refuses to enjoy life because we have survived when our loved one has not. Again, it is a way of quietly punishing ourselves. This is a tendency which suicide survivors have.

Your departed loved-one would not want you to live a diminished life because of them.

While it is a form of self-care to allow ourselves to feel the tremendously torturous feelings that come with being a suicide survivor, it's easy to become mired in them, ruminating on our losses. Eventually we can become so battle-fatigued that we don't have the strength to start a new enterprise, go after new relationships, or even to set new goals. It's less effort to sit on the safe sidelines of life than be the center of attention; less effort to live in the shadow of the past than have to re-create ourselves.

In fact, few things are harder than re-creating ourselves. Although I came to see that I was not the cause of my daughter's decision to end her life, one of the most crucial and powerful components of my healing process was when I took a fearless look at what I did well as a parent, and also where I failed to be the parent I wanted to be. Alcoholics Anonymous has a 12-step program that most people have heard about, and the fourth step in overcoming an addiction is to make "a searching and fearless moral inventory of ourselves" (AA Publishing, 1981.) But rather than playing the blame game with yourself, try to remember the old saying: No one is perfect. Acknowledge that in owning your shortcomings, you are stronger than when you didn't.

As you perform your moral inventory, don't compare yourself to others. Your fingerprint, voiceprint and even the iris of your eyes are unique and can't be duplicated; proof that you were meant to be different. If you feel alone or misunderstood, it's because existentially speaking, you are! We humans like to be in relationship with others, but there's a part of each of us that will always feel different, and that's what you'll have to come to terms with. This is something Mo didn't understand, and I wish I had spent more time talking with her about it. She was biracial, and always said she didn't fit in: not with the white kids because she looked black, and not with the black kids because she had white mannerisms. She was caught between two worlds ethnically, and the ambiguity and uncertainty of it caused feelings of insecurity in her. She also felt she was not thin enough to be accepted by the girls at her high school, so she stopped taking her anti-depressant, because one of the side effects is weight gain. A deadly decision.

Yes, I wish I had talked to her about this.

CHAPTER TEN

THE MEANING OF DEATH HAS CHANGED FOR ME. I don't fear it anymore; rather, I see it as the natural progression of the soul, the next step of life. In the words of a near-death experiencer, a woman named Willie Mae whose story is published in the book, *Blessings in Disguise*, (2000) by Barbara R. Rommer, M.D., "The soul doesn't die. The body's a transporter. There is something within that's the real person... I believe that there are other worlds and when you've progressed enough, you go higher. You keep going and going until you perfect yourself. You keep coming back until you're perfect." Patrick, another near-death experiencer, says basically the same thing: "We don't die. The physical body is merely a vessel that we temporarily occupy for the purpose of working out the lessons that we are presented with on this plane. It's like if you rent a car for a trip. When you finish the trip you return the car, and when it's time to take another trip, you rent another car. Of course there's sadness at someone's death, because they're not physically here for you to touch. But if you live on the East Coast and call an aunt that lives in California on the phone, you're not physically touching her either. When someone dies, they're also just a long distance phone call away!"

Many of the grieving clients I worked with confided that it helped them enormously to "talk to" the deceased as if they were talking on the phone with them. Not only was it an opportunity to express the feelings they had stored up, but they described sensing the presence of their deceased love-one during these one-way conversations. Since Mo's death I've come to believe that loved ones on the other side can hear when the "phone's ringing" for them, and do listen in. After the first year I didn't feel her presence as acutely as I had. But in the moments I miss her and need her help, I trust that our line of communication is always open and she will respond. Ours is a bond that will never be broken. When she first passed I believe she was earth-bound, or more accurately, she was bound to me (and other family members), and our house where she had passed. That first year was like living in a psychic storm—a spiritual battlefield. The energy was so palpable and intense that it was often frightening, uncomfortable and frustrating to live there. Both Rachael and I experienced the distinct feeling of being watched. Late at night I would wake to strange, unexplainable noises that sounded like things being dropped or the sound of someone walking in the next room. We also would see white flashes, or what looked like white mist, that would appear and disappear in the blink of an eye, zipping by as fast as a lighting strike.

This may sound strange but I feel closer now to my daughter than when she was alive. It's almost as if we've forged a new bond, a more equal and honest relationship, an adult relationship now that she's "grown up" in Spirit. I often sense when she has dropped by for a mother-daughter reminisce. One morning an acquaintance of mine who is intuitive invited her friends on her social website page to ask any question they had of her for free. I couldn't resist—free is a good price. I asked her a question about my professional life which she answered with astounding accuracy. Then she added, "And I see a butterfly around you." I smiled. The butterfly was my symbol for Moriyah. This was because just several days after her passing, I was sitting in the sun on the porch, weeping, pleading with God to send me a sign that Moriyah had passed to the other side safely. There was such a deep black void in my heart–I had to know, absolutely had to know that my little girl was alright. As I thought this, a monarch butterfly flitted by, doing flip flops in front of me. I had never seen a monarch butterfly before–they're not common in Oregon. Could this be a sign? *It's just a coincidence*, said my skeptic mind. I sat there puffing on my cigarette and thought, *I'm gonna need more than that, God*. To my surprise, the Monarch came back, swooping and soaring so close it nearly knocked me over. I laughed, and then I cried. This magnificent symbol of transformation had appeared out of nowhere, and seemed to be Moriyah saying, "Look Mom, I made it. I'm transformed, and I'm free!"

After the intuitive told me she saw a butterfly around me, I went for a walk with Romeo and prayed, "Moriyah, if you're still around me, could you send a butterfly again as a sign?" I knew it was a little presumptuous, but it had been over a year since I'd seen the butterfly, and I was missing my daughter terribly that day. That night I awoke at 3:00 am and heard a faint tinny noise in the kitchen. I didn't think much of it and went back to sleep. I got up the next morning and went to get my morning coffee. As I did I stepped on something and looked down to see it was the metal butterfly magnet which had been stuck at the top of the refrigerator. I asked Rachael if she had been to the fridge and accidently knocked it down that morning, and she said no. Did it *fly* down on its own? I don't see how.

The next day I was visiting someone and was admiring her vegetable garden, when all of a sudden another monarch butterfly turned the corner and landed on a tomato plant and sat, slowly fanning its wings; it was huge, it was almost the size of my hand, majestic and breathtaking.

I did some research and learned that although their lifespan is short, they migrate up to 2,400 miles. That's a long journey in a short time! A very fitting message from a girl who only lived 15 years. Several days after I saw the Monarchs for the second time, my intuitive friend posted this message: "Just when the caterpillar thought the world was over, it became a butterfly."

Of course I'm aware that butterflies appearing, birds tapping on my window, electronics turning on and off at will, and all the other unexplainable occurrences are not scientifically verifiable proof of after-death contacts. A doctor named Elisa Medhus never believed in life after death either. As an accomplished physician, she placed her faith squarely in science. Her parents were staunch atheists and physicians. She came from a distinguished line of hardened skeptics. All of that changed after her son Erik took his own life. After a number of what Dr. Medhus felt were after-death communications, she found a medium who was able to bring through detailed confirmation and messages from Erik. She chronicled her story in *Conversations with My Son in the Afterlife* (Beyond Words, 2013).

There are broken people who become more beautiful for the brokenness; like the allegory of *The Velveteen Rabbit*, they look worn and tattered on the outside, but the light on the inside outshines the wrinkles and the battered exterior. If you were to interview these people they would tell you, in essence, that their wisdom is nothing more than healed pain. Like the Velveteen Rabbit, whose quest it was to become real through the love of his owner, we become real (genuine, sincere and authentic) when we have suffered. The Velveteen Rabbit learns that "Real isn't how you are made. It's a thing that happens to you. When a child loves you for a long, long time, not just to play with, but really loves you, then you have become real."

Pretending is the opposite of being real. Pretense is a low-level of functioning. When we feel insignificant and common-place, we put on a show and talk up our worth. But once you have been broken, truly cracked in half and broken wide open, you see who you are and who you aren't. The need to brag goes away, leaving humility and an unshakable understanding, a quiet confidence, of who you really are, your true worth. Again, this process takes time. Slow down. Take the time. You're not going to stop grieving, but you can't move forward until you release negative emotions of blame and anger.

Suzi the psychic's message from my daughter was *I'm sorry for the mess I left*, and when she said it, my mind went to the bedroom with the clothes on the floor and hair in the bathroom sink; but of course that's not what Moriyah meant. Yes, her suicide left a big mess. But as soon as she acknowledged it, any residual anger I felt for her vanished. Holding on to anger will stop you in your tracks and you won't be able to move forward even an inch. Learn to forgive. But it's not going to happen overnight. It's all process.

CHAPTER ELEVEN

MY FAVORITE DEFINITION OF LOVE comes from Harry Palmer: "Love is the willingness to create a space for change to occur," (1986) and that includes self-love. For many people dealing with the suicide of a family member, self-love isn't possible until forgiveness happens. We need to remember that forgiveness is not erasing what was; forgiveness, like love, is being willing to create something new. Forgiveness doesn't mean we forget the past. It means we no longer allow it to control our life. We also need to forgive the loved one who gave up.

For me, an unexpected consequence of Mo's suicide was that, in addition to blaming myself, I discovered that some people blamed me, too. I have a friend who has not spoken to me since it happened; clearly, she holds me responsible. Research has shown that this is often the case, and it's something we need to be prepared for, without taking it upon ourselves as validation that the suicide was our fault. Let them have their feelings, but don't let them tear down all the healing work you've accomplished.

There's a powerful concept called, "Radical Acceptance" in *Dialectical Behavioral Therapy* (DBT) that's applicable here. Creator of DBT Dr. Marsha Linnehan (herself a mental health survivor) says, "One of the four options you have for any problem is Radical Acceptance" (1993). What is it? Radical means complete and total.

When you've radically accepted, a heart change occurs. All of you is listening instead of fighting. All of you is open instead of defensive. It is a complete and total transformation of your outlook, and results in peace, gratitude, even joy. It doesn't mean you try to forget what happened, it's not a giant eraser. It means you accept that suffering is part of life–part of *your* life–but it doesn't have to define you. Radical Acceptance allows you to feel the sadness but move on. I miss my daughter and think of her every day; I always will. But I gave myself a window of time (for me, a year) in which to work through my insecurity and find a new place for myself in this world. By working through grief and growing out of mourning, I've determined not to stay stuck in a lifetime of unhappiness–I know Moriyah wouldn't want that for me.

I've made other momentous and positive changes in my life: hypnotherapy and my writing. I'm still working as a healer, but in an environment with less emotional triggers for me.

Recently I was watching a forensic show, and they interviewed the father of a teen who'd been brutally murdered. He said, *It doesn't get better over time. For parents of children who have died, it gets worse over time, if anything.* There was footage of him brooding over pictures of his daughter, and while I certainly can relate to missing my daughter more each day, it hasn't been my experience that it gets worse. I really believe that even in the most tragic of deaths, even suicides and murders, time can bring healing. What the TV show didn't say was whether this grieving father had reached out for support or not. Had he gone to counseling to work through his feelings? Had he joined a grief support group, where he could be assured that he wasn't alone in his struggle? Did he discuss it regularly with a loved one, telling his story and expressing his pain, anger and anguish over and over again so he felt heard and understood? Did he read books which helped him to understand and process the grief? Did he use prayer or meditation to express his suffering and receive divine insight and healing? My guess is that he's trapped in his suffering, and hasn't done the time consuming grief work necessary to fully recover.

A little over a year after Moriah's death, Rachael and I were having what I called "stand-offs." We didn't fight, we just weren't relating anymore. It was if she had gone to her corner and I had gone to mine. In the evenings and on weekends she played video games and I kept my nose buried in my work. We had evolved into roommates who kissed good morning and good night, discussed the bills, had dinner, and watched the TV news together. We didn't brooch the subject of a withering sex life and the passion we'd once had, but we both knew the love-at-first-sight magic had evaporated.

In my professional experience I'd determined that there are two kinds of couples: those who voiced their opinions and who argued and fought vehemently. I called them "the louds." They could get ugly with name calling and biting sarcasm. But in the end, they tended to resolve their issues. Sometimes they stayed together and other times they agreed to go their separate ways, but they had the guts to do the work. The second kind of couple, obviously, were "the quiets." They could also be called "the avoiders" because that's what they devoted most of their energy to. They avoided talking, avoided intimacy, avoided confrontation, avoided connecting on any level. Typically there would be years of silence, and then one would announce "suddenly" that he or she wanted out, or was having an affair. The quiets sometimes got close to understanding their dynamics, and then would stop coming to therapy; unwilling to admit that with honesty might come divorce.

Surprisingly, with Rachael and me, I turned out to be a quiet. Although I had faith in our ability to work through our issues with the help of a counselor, I was the one who didn't want to go. I told Rachael that I knew what the questions would be, and that I already knew the answers. I wanted Rachael to go, and figure out why *she* had stopped relating to me, why our sex life had flown out the window, and why, as she put it, "she couldn't feel anything" since Moriyah's death. She refused to go alone.

Then it hit me: the reason I didn't want to go was because I didn't want to hear the hard stuff, the stuff that might hurt. Just like I backed down when it came to dragging Mo to counseling. So I suggested to Rachael that instead of going to counseling, we bare our souls and be completely honest with each other. I wanted her to understand what I had been going through, and I wanted her to tell me exactly how she was feeling. It took months of intense and sometimes angry dialogue before we finally began to see through each other's eyes.

A few years ago I heard a motivational speaker point out the similarity between the words "sacred" and "scared." So in order to transform scared into sacred, here are the lessons I needed to learn:

Treasure the relationships in your life

It seemed I never knew who I was unless I was embroiled in a relationship. My romantic partners were my validation that I was somebody, that I was worthy to be loved. My father had not been able to validate me as a girl, and my mother had been unable to validate me as a woman when I came out. In the spaces between relationships I was nervous, tense and insecure. I would re-focus on my daughter during my single phases, and while I tried to make her my focus, while I relished every minute of snuggle and play time that we shared, there was always that empty, gnawing, terrible reminder in the pit of my stomach that I didn't exist and that my life had no meaning without a romantic partner. When I had a partner the world was a fiesta: colorful and exciting, thrilling and new. When I was just a struggling single mom the world turned black, white and cold again. It drained of color and each day I lived in the expectancy of the next romance. I had to have it like addicts have to have their heroin. I couldn't see myself then. I was blinded by my own desperate need to be important to someone, and didn't realize that my attention turned away from my daughter each time a bright and shiny new woman came into my life. I never meant to leave her behind. I just couldn't see her over the growing pile of my own insecurities. While I included her in all my activities—"It's a package deal," I'd tell prospective girlfriends—the main event was someone else, always someone else. I see it all so clearly now: I had no center. And while she knew I loved her, I know she did, and while I always tried to include her, the truth is, she was along for the ride and not the center of my stage. When I think of how I dragged her through school after school, move after move, through a string of partners, I want to scream into the emptiness, "I am so, so sorry." And this is the miserable life lesson I learned too late; I took her for granted. I thought she was mine and she'd always be here to love me in her quiet way, and to contradict me the way teenagers do. I thought I had time to work it out, and time for our wounds to heal. Why don't we say what needs to be said? We are hostages to fear, cowards who hide behind busyness and responsibilities—mute and proud, yet stopped and impotent. I wish I had appreciated the treasure shimmering before me.

Matter doesn't matter, so discover what does

"Things" won't amount to a hill of beans when you think about how you invested your time. There's nothing wrong with having nice things; you don't have to take a vow of poverty. But when "stuff" is what you're primarily focused upon, if your self-worth is based on your "image" and your wealth, you've missed the point, because it could all be swept away tomorrow. People are the only valuables. Be willing to release "stuff" (and even your image) in exchange for developing sacred places inside of you. My concept of God has been forever altered because of Mo's suicide. I used to think in conventional terms about God: you were good or you were bad, and if you were bad, God punished you. And sometimes God punished you even when you thought you were good, and you weren't meant to understand. "The problem of pain," is what renowned Christian scholar C.S. Lewis called Atheism's most potent argument against a Supreme Being: if God is all-powerful, He would not allow good people to suffer. Author Deepak Chopra counters, "The question of why God allows bad things to happen isn't a simple human question… it's a spiritual question." In other words, to reduce God to a "human being in disguise" is too simplistic; and yet that is how so many of us were raised–projecting our human values and traits and neuroses onto God. The Buddha taught that we are broken so we can become enlightened. This is what the Buddha taught. *Dukkha*, the Buddhist word for suffering, can also be translated as anxiety, stress, or unsatisfactoriness. Buddha's Four Noble Truths explains that suffering results from holding too tightly to that which was never ours in the first place. It reminds us that everything is only temporary. Especially all that "stuff" we find ourselves attached to.

AFTERWARD

IT'S BEEN A YEAR AND A HALF since Mo's death, and I'm going through some of my stuff, and find this in one of my journals:

Since Moriyah's death I've kept myself
from journaling or blogging, which is
my normal method of artistic
expression. Perhaps I don't want to see
my feelings splattered on paper. I
still can't sleep at night. I stay up
as long as I possibly can, as if
there's only one day left to live and
my inner clock knows I'm running out of
time. Her death reminded me,
poignantly, how short our time is. My
brain thinks it's not safe or
permissible to go to sleep, because had
I not gone to sleep that fateful night,
perhaps she would still be alive. Even
though people tell me I'm not to blame,
that vigilant voice constantly,
persistently reminds me, like a

mother's finger being wagged at me,
that it's most definitely not safe to
sleep. I'm overwhelmed with exhaustion.

Her death caused me to re-examine my own
life, and to re-assess everything I
thought I knew about me. The morning of
her suicide, a giant malevolent hand
caught me by the foot, turned me upside
down and began shaking so hard that
everything I thought I was, including
all my self importance, arrogance and
narcissism tumbled out. For a while I
lost my mind. I'm not sure I'll ever
regain the person I once was, and
certain I don't want to. I think I hate
that person now. It remains to be seen
how to take nothing and construct a
life of it again. A part of me will
always suffer because of her choice.

The first three weeks are a blur. Two
days after having found her, I remember
vomiting upon waking, a delayed
reaction. I was in shock and I didn't
know it. I found it odd at the time,
vomiting when I didn't feel ill. I
wasn't cognizant whether it was night
or day, the weekday or weekend. When
you're in shock, day-to-day rituals
lose their meaning. I was disoriented,
walking with wooden legs and the
feeling of being mildly concussed. When

people talked to me, it seemed they
were talking *at* me, throwing words at
my head that I had to dodge, because I
couldn't make sense of what they were
saying. I stumbled around this way, in
a daze, not hearing or seeing anything
for three weeks. I was often
dissociated from my body. When it's too
painful to stay in the body, the mind
compassionately allows you to withdraw.
I stayed outside myself looking in from
a more comfortable distance, in a
perpetual state of numb.

A part of me will never accept that she
is gone. I cannot accept her death, it
would be heinous of me to accept it,
for then I would have to say goodbye,
something a mother cannot do. She used
to go to her father's for the summers.
I would put on a brave face until she
had gotten on the train and we'd waved
goodbye. Then I would cry, unseen, on
the way home. But I could stop crying
because I knew she'd be coming back
when the leaves began to turn colors
and fall from the trees, when it was
time to go school shopping together.
There was a predictable ending and
beginning, life was certain. My mind
won't let me cry too much because it's
waiting for her to step off the train,
a little taller and slightly more grown

up than when she left; a whole summer
away is a tragedy for a mother. But
there's no train, and there's no
Moriyah. Everything keeps fooling me.

A part of me will always persecute me.
The part that doesn't want me to sleep
is the most stubbornly problematic. You
can go without eating, but you can't go
without sleeping. I think it's
torturing me. I'm terrified I might see
her in my dreams. What if I see her
suffering for what she did? She
suffered enough in life, more than most
people. She was severely depressed
since the age of eleven, having watched
her father be mummified in his own skin
by ALS, and then being torn from his
side at his death. I can't bear the
thought that God would let her suffer
in death. I don't believe she should
suffer because she was mentally ill.
You can't help an illness. She didn't
want to die this way. But most people
don't see depression as an illness.
Even though science has shown that
depression is frequently a lethal
diagnosis, suicide is still condemned
by churches as worthy of eternal
damnation, and talked about by some who
stand with upturned noses as if the
person deserves to be condemned. I
wonder if they had to live day in and

day out, trapped in a hopelessly
tortured mind, would they be so quick
to pass judgment?

She got the depressive gene from me,
from my side of the family. The curse
of depression has overshadowed my whole
life. My first bout with depression
started in my thirties, and steadily
grew worse every year until it became
crippling, disabling me until I found
myself living in my parent's attic,
jobless and homeless at the age of 40.
It didn't matter that I had a degree in
psychology. Mental illness doesn't care
what you know. It will tear up anyone's
life, it's no respecter of persons.
Mental illness can beat you to a pulp,
crushing your dreams until the
certainty and fight you once had is
only a foggy memory, and it will grin
as it wipes your life away.

I hate the ticking of the clocks and the
morbid quiet, ringing loudly in my
ears. There is too much time now, and
an uncertainty of what's to come. Life
has been paused, as if stillborn. Days
are interminably too long, living in
fear and in loathing of my fear. Nights
are the longest, waking ceaselessly
with a tight terror in my chest. I
begin to cry and my throat ceases up,

catches like I'm strangling, gasping
for air like a fish out of water. She
died hurting and gasping like this.
It's as if I'm trying to strangle
myself with tears. If I go to sleep she
will die all over again, and I'll only
awaken to a nightmare. To avoid this
terrible choking business I catch and
stop myself before crying, tears so
deeply suppressed that all that's left
of my soul is this creaky door, this
rusty gate flapping in the wind. My
voice sounds like a squeaky wheel-
dilapidated, fragile and broken as I
have never heard myself sound.
Certainly your child's suicide cannot
beat you? But on that dreadful day, in
that grim, hellish moment when life
became a nightmare, my soul stopped
singing. And so the blackbird, now she
sings for me.

I know what it is to be stripped of
everything dear. In one moment, in one
lightning strike - stripped of the
courage to try. I live day to day
because if everything can be taken I
ought to live with an open palm. If I
don't grasp anything it can't be stolen
from me. My life was once a veritable
garden, colorful and alive, jammed with
ideas I'd never get to. But then the
atom bomb was detonated. Everything is

still dead. How can there be anything
but death? Life was decimated,
destroyed in the fallout.
It's true that I don't hope for anything
anymore. I built my life on being a
savior. Now I can't even save myself.

Anniversaries and holidays are dreaded
occasions. You're moving along in a
straight line, feeling as if you may
have gotten your sea legs when out of
nowhere comes a holiday, knocking you
down, reminding you that she's not
there. She's the empty chair at the
table that everyone's avoiding looking
at. Her 16th birthday is coming, and I
don't even know where to begin. I want
to buy a sweet sixteen birthday card
that catches my eye in the postal
store, but I don't know who I'm buying
it for - me or her? Does she know it's
her birthday? Can she see me standing
frozen in the store, not knowing if
it's healthy or unhealthy to buy your
dead daughter a birthday card that
she's never going to see? My life is
full of these awkward moments, like
being asked how many kids I have. I
have three kids, but one of them
passed, I say quickly, as if by saying
it quicker it will lessen the impact.
And will I ever become accustomed to
condolences? In a way it's comforting,

having people say they're sorry, and it's affirming as they swear they could never live through losing a child. Oh, you'd live through it, I think, you'd just wish you hadn't. I've begged God to take me in my most desperate hours. I imagined scenarios of misfortune in which there was a head-on collision and I didn't survive. Or I stepped in front of a speeding train. When agony and fear plague you, you toy with the idea of death, or perhaps death toys with you. If you flirt with the idea long enough it begins to look more and more attractive. Anything hideous can look attractive if you court it long enough. This is what she must have done: she must have stared at death for so long that the gruesomeness of it melted away, and the truth wrapped carefully inside it seemed all at once apparent to her, like a gift. Yet even in my darkest moments I've always had a strong appetite for life. I decide to get the birthday card. I write her a poem, and enclose it, a mother's sentiments entombed forever in a .99 cent card, which seems fitting-what I wished to say is once again buried. This wasn't the way it was supposed to be, a cheap card and a poem on your 16th birthday. I wish you would come back for one day, just one glorious day. I'd

celebrate you like I should have. I'd
make you listen until I confessed it
all-how I'm dying inside, a little each
day, just as the trees shed their
leaves, one by one until they are
barren, inconsolable, and nobody can
say they didn't cry.

I must muster what seems like courage to
go on without you, yet courage hasn't
the slightest thing to do with carrying
on. On the outside it looks as if I've
forgotten and somehow gotten past it,
while reality so jarred me loose that I
stopped living a long time ago. I am
only going through the motions, you
see. Living is now like bathing -
something I have to do to keep from
smelling bad. But your corpse was my
corpse; I buried me with you. So any
living, or the ridiculous idea of
triumph is a soul dummy that I've
propped up for the world to marvel at.
It keeps the vultures at bay.

My hair has begun to turn grey. I don't
know if this is due to the trauma I've
been through or not, but it does seem
like the grey hair came on all of a
sudden. That's another reprehensible
fact about surviving a suicide:
everything that goes wrong you seem to
blame on the suicide. First it was my

financial troubles, which I had plenty
of, directly relatable to her death.
Next my newlywed sex life was
torpedoed. I mean, sex is a celebration
of life, is it not? How can I celebrate
when I am still in mourning? Then my
business went down the tubes, because I
couldn't stand to listen to one more
client complain to me about their
divorce or their bratty kid which
seemed completely inconsequential by
comparison. But then I began to layer
other problems on top of the heap,
attributing it all to trauma. I've
become my own private version of a
hypochondriac, which I utterly disdain.
I like to watch Woody Allen movies, but
I don't want to *be* a Woody Allen movie.
Yet trauma has a way of doing this to
you. It creates a mild paranoia, as if
you're waiting for the next ax to fall,
seeing your misfortune played out in
unrelated events. Any rational person
would look at my circumstances and say
that I just need to relax. Yet
unfortunate circumstances do not breed
a sane relaxation about the future. I
want very much to stay calm, and to
cultivate a spiritual serenity about
me. After all, this is what saints and
martyrs do. They rise above it,
elevating themselves above mortal
tragedy, transcending all the petty and

disagreeable emotions, portraying a
stalwart façade, forgetting about their
troubles completely as they rush to aid
of those less fortunate. But wasn't
that what got me in trouble in the
first place? Haven't I regretted, a
hundred thousand times over, being too
busy caring for others, having missed
the signs of my own daughter's demise?
And there I go again, round-robining
back to her death - I am a saint lying
sanctimoniously atop a pyre of
unfortunate circumstances.

I am ruined. Ruined like a woman whose
unfaithful husband leaves her out of
his thoughts when he goes to be with
his mistress. Her note said she was
leaving to be with her father who had
passed. That she missed him. Just like
that. As if what I gave her, although
imperfect, was wholly inadequate. In
every criticism lies a seed of truth.
And by the truth you are crushed, you
are crucified, for you know about how
wishful thinking was more real than
your wasted courage, and how she took
your hand, outstretched, only in a
dream. It is not the betrayals which
crucify us; it is the terror of
rejection which we harbor. Our own
words betray us, our own fear stops us
up. She betrayed me, she left me… but

hadn't we said our goodbyes long ago? A sin of omission rather than commission - waiting for the right time that would never come. Women of ruin let their hair go grey, letting the foolish and naïve dreams slip through their lifeless fingers, letting their surety go slack, letting life be not what they were told, but what they were left with. I feel more like a widow than a bereaved parent. How can you not love your own child more than a lover? A lover is separate, while your children hold a piece of your soul in their charming smile, their awkward gate, and in a thousand other ways. I used to tease her that only her toes and her ears were like mine - all the rest she got from her dad. It seemed she was born to be his soul mate. Two quiet, gentle doves who paired the instant they locked eyes. When he died, it was then that her soul departed. She returned to me in mourning - a broken, hostile, withered shell. The girl I saw off for the summers on the train never returned. The suicide was the formal notice, her announcement that her heart had in fact stopped beating, and she had lived the morbid life of a corpse. Her room was proof of this - a shambles, stuffed with rancid dishes, filthy clothes and sketches of nooses

and devils. She had become a mute
lunatic and wandered into enemy
territory. I suffer the most when I
consider how frightfully
lonely she must have been in death. She
was ruined years before I was, and one
day she remembered the songs of her
Negro ancestors. They were singing to
her about the promised - land, a land
flowing with milk and honey, and her
daddy was there, just waitin' on her,
singing to her the old hymnal, "Leaning
on the Everlasting Arms," the one I
used to sing to her at night as a baby
to get her to go to sleep. She used to
beg me, even as an older child, to sing
her that song, as if she already knew
what it meant.

After reading it, I sit back and ponder my progress. Yes, I've come a long, long way. And if I've learned one thing, it's this: Life is a dream we will awaken from one morning. We will look back on it–maybe in delight, maybe in horror–then we will leave it behind. The way a butterfly sheds its cocoon, we will forget it ever held us captive. We are all ghosts in one another's dream, and the only thing that makes life real is love. Love is the awakening. I was awakened by loving her.

References:

Blake, J. (2011). *Do loved ones bid farewell from beyond the grave?* CNN Living. Retrieved from: www.cnn.com/2011/09/23/living/crisisapparitions/

Fredrickson, B. (2009). *Positivity: Groundbreaking Research Reveals How to Embrace the Hidden Strength of Positive Emotions, Overcome Negativity, and Thrive.* Random House, LLC, New York, NY.

Lewis, C.S. (2009). *A Grief Observed.* HarperCollins Publishers, US.

Linnehan, M. (1993). *Skills Training Manual for Treating Borderline Personality Disorder.* The Guilford Press, New York, NY.

Maslow, A. (1943). "Theories of Human Motivation." *Psychological Review*, Vol. 50(4).

Medhus, E. (2013). *My Son and the Afterlife: Conversations from The Other Side.* Atria Books/Beyond Words Publishing, Hillsboro, OR.

Palmer, H. (1986). "Beyond the Buddhic Path with Avatar". *Avatar Master-Wizard Harry Palmer speaks.* Archived from the original on 200703-27.

Plath, S. (1963). *The Bell Jar.* Heinemann, England.

Rommer, B. (2000). *Blessing in Disguise: Another Side of The Near-Death Experience.* Llewellyn Publications, St. Paul, MN.

Seibert, A. (2005). *The Resiliency Advantage: Master Change, Thrive Under Pressure, and Bounce Back from Setbacks.* Berrett-Koehler Publishers, San Francisco, CA.

Theisen, D., Matera, D. (2001). *Childlight: How Children Reach Out To Their Parents from the Beyond*. Far Hills, N.J.: New Horizon Press.

Williams, M. (1922). *The Velveteen Rabbit (or How Toys Become Real)*. George H. Doran Company, New York, NY.

19373651R00064

Made in the USA
San Bernardino, CA
24 February 2015